DEGAS

Jean-Jacques Lévêque

DEGAS

CRESCENT BOOKS
NEW YORK

Translated from the French by *Carol Lee Rathman*

This 1990 edition published by Crescent Books,
distributed by Crown Publishers, Inc., 225 Park Avenue South,
New York, New York 10003.

Printed and bound in Italy

ISBN 0-517-69481-6

h g f e d c b a

Table of contents

Index of illustrations

Boulevard Rochechouart and Rue Clignancourt.
(photo by R. Viollet)

INTRODUCTION

The first nationwide festival to celebrate the Third Republic was held on July 14, 1880.

The attraction that garnered the most attention was the review at Longchamp, which immortalized an eminently silly patriotic song on everyone's tongue at the time.

In those days, people would break into song at the drop of a hat. At the Chat Noir in Boulevard Rochechouart, Radolph Salis drew crowds from all over Paris, eager to witness the reinstatement of the French ditty.

In 1885 the cabaret moved to Rue de Laval (today's Rue de Douai) and here, amid the somewhat tasteless mock-medieval décor of the new club, people of all classes picked at cherries steeped in brandy and obligingly allowed their clothes to be slashed to shreds. Garbed in long black gloves, Yvette Guilbert conducted these extravagant evening *divertissements*, cutting a strange and ambiguous figure as she weaved her way among the guests, reciting saucy verses in her biting and sometimes vulgar tones.

Monday night was reserved for the Opéra. Tuesdays one went to the Café Français, Fridays to the Cirque... The entire city was busy amusing itself.

Along the Champs Elysées, between one infamous pleasure-house and the next one could sometimes find the occasional quiet corner.

Then there was the Palais de Glace where, keen to cut a dapper figure, innumerable men gathered at five in the afternoon, each with a girl or two on his arm plucked from the little groups who clustered in trepidation at the rink's edge, hoping for a chance invitation. Meanwhile, a short distance away at the Mabille, the throng danced their feet off. And outside, just off Allée des Veuves (today's Avenue Montaigne) there is a small "accursed" garden where, according to some mothers, the "serpent of temptation" was said to lurk.

The glistening gaslit streetlights and venetian lanterns wrought with zinc palms shed their light with complicity on the milling crowd out for easy thrills and gratification.

From Degas' sketchbook

The deafening strains of music echoed through the whole of Paris, as it expanded along its new boulevards bequeathed by the Empire and their architect Monsieur Hausmann.

New constructions began to fill the vacant lots around the as yet unsullied white stone railway stations. The brand new Trocadero stood quite alone, out in the wilds of the orchards and kitchen gardens. Auteuil was leagues away. Only the de Goncourts were eccentric enough to settle so far from civilization. Monsieur Edmond, the only remaining heir, did not find the enduring peace and quiet he sought – his repose was trespassed by the crowing of the cockerels, the rhythmic banging of the smithy's hammer, the song and clamor of the local boys.

And then in 1871, this corner of the countryside was suddenly made accessible by a branch of the railway. Two hardy carthorses pulled a tram fairly bursting with passengers. In those days, traveling by rail was a safer bet than braving the uneven roads. Twenty-five years later, the horses would be put out to graze and the carriages were drawn by a steam-engine.

From the very outset, the trams sported an upper deck. To get up there you had to be young, sprightly, prepared to risk your neck, though, for reasons of decorum, this display of agility was not expected of the ladies. Later, members of the gentler sex were able to mount the metal stair that spiraled to the upper deck, showing off their gaudy little umbrellas and other seasonal accoutrements.

Movement in those days was unhurried, as the rhythms of life were fashionably slow.

No other means of transport was yet available. It was not until 1900 that the first line of the Métro was opened to the public.

Until then, those who wished to venture "out of town" could hire a bateau mouche for a quarter of a franc from Charenton to Suresnes. Times were changing. The rich began to desert the private mansions with their costly gardens and courtyards in favor of apartments. The tall carriage entrance became a sign of status and wealth, a sign of resistance. A single door was open admittance of family decline. Meanwhile, inside, the furniture was dominated by the *armoire* with its ponderous mirror, and by the pianoforte, a sign of learning.

As for literature, the entire city seemed to be absorbed in some cheap novel or other.

But this somnolence was broken by the primordial tonality of Richard Wagner, whose music suddenly found its way into the Sunday program at the Cirque d'Hiver.

Guests were received with a dutiful display of airs and graces, people were respectfully bored by family life.

Personal hygiene was not a national *forte*. The baths – for those who had them – were nothing like the baths of today. "Two swan's beaks disgorged water into an enameled zinc tub which was then heated." Consequently, most people made do with a small basin filled with water heated on the kitchen stove.

The body was a source of general shame or embarrassment. Mirrors were kept out of sight and there were no places of ablution. In contrast, great pride was taken in the head and clothes and the advent of photography offered yet another occasion to pose, supercilious and filled with dignity.

The infant was followed by the churchman or soldier, the young bride and the happy groom by the venerable forebear.

Photography was a new sensation, and wherever a photographer demonstrated his equipment he caused quite a stir. In the countryside, he was considered a kind of magician.

In Paris, photographers required a license from the Constabulary to practice their trade in the streets.

No one guessed that a revolution was about to take place behind the black veil of the photographer. His magic plates revealed not only what the eye could see, but also what it could not see.

Blvd. des Capucines
(photo by R. Viollet)

Montmartre – Café restaurant in Place Blanche, around 1900.
(photo by R. Viollet)

BOUGEREAU

JEAN BÉRAUD

CORMON

CAROLUS DURAN

The first pictures of horses showed up the errors in equestrian paintings and the spread of the new medium caused painters to completely reinvent their art.

High above the chatter of the crowds in the pavement cafés, sipping their ubiquitous absinthe, the shrill cry of the newspaper vendors could be heard and suddenly the stuffy Paris air was filled with a new topic and source of gossip as the public quickly took sides on the Dreyfus affair.

Families were divided, the younger generation turned against the authority, insolence and sectarian mentality of the previous generation. While the columns of the daily *Le Temps* offered the more serious members of the community a moderate version of the events and *Le Figaro* claimed to represent the true Parisian, *Le Gaulois*, with its devoted readership of social climbers, title-seekers and other aspirants to acquired nobility, reported on weddings and other society gatherings with a cunning compilation of the going "Who's Who."

Socialites mentioned were very sensitive and when a name was misspelled, the maligned reader was likely to cancel his subscription.

Petit Journal and *Petit Parisien* wasted little time on such political subtleties and preferred the gore and passion of the city's crime, looking for quantity not quality in their readership.

The *Le Matin* and the *Le Journal* went for a more speedy reportage typical of the American press.

In the meantime, advertising began to get a foothold everywhere. Then the press opened its pages to literature, documenting the vicissitudes of the great writers of the times–at seventy, Victor Hugo continued to occupy the throne of the French literary pantheon, while Flaubert, who occasionally strayed into Paris from his country retreat on the Seine, died suddenly, leaving *Bouvard et Pécouch et* unfinished, a work in which all Paris was to recognize itself.

Dumas *fils* was the unchallenged sovereign of the theater, much to the chagrin of naturalist author Edmond de Goncourt, who consoled himself by keeping an open salon that attracted all the literary pundits of the day.

Under the worldly guidance of Alphonse Daudet and Emile Zola, the meetings unfolded in an aura of veiled sophism and intrigue.

Not far away in the musty rooms of an apartment in Rue de Rome, a respectful audience was pondering the enigmatic utterances of a new young wordmonger, Stéphane Mallarmé.

Anatole France, a reader at the publishers Lemerre (the biggest alongside Charpentier) was also beginning to attract a following. In the midst of this paper empire, military painter Meissonnier looked on with self-satisfaction and stroked his beard. His refined and smooth paintings had found favor, as had the "Renaissance-type" nudes of Bouguereau and the patriotism of Detaille and Alphonse de Neuville, who sculpted family tombs on commission.

Léon Bonnat and Carolus Duran shared their clientele of celebrities, titled gentry and ministers, not to mention the Presidents of the Republic themselves.

A BOURGEOIS GENTILHOMME

During the eighteen year reign of Louis Philippe (1830-1848), bankers were the absolute dispensers of credit. Rather than speculators, they were capable jugglers of funds. The public leaned on them for advice and help, as did the Government. The first public loan came later in 1852, although there were no large banks as such in France until 1860. Bankers enjoyed the considerable esteem of the grateful public. But they also knew how to act with prudence and judgment.

More often than not, banks were family enterprises and their outlets were modest in appearance: *"There were no offices as such, and the public was received in the banker's studio. In order to convey a sense of trust and reassure clients that their money was not being squandered, the banker was obliged to give an impression of great parsimony in affairs. The minimal staff of these studios was employed in copying. The office head received the banker's clients personally and also served as his confidant[1]".*

Together with the doctor and the curate, the banker was a trusted friend of the family and Monsieur de Gas was no exception. He possessed all the innate characteristics of his genre: he was well-read, a lover of music and a passionate admirer of the fine arts. These attributes were to be a major influence in the vocation and future of his son Edgar. Edgar Degas' character and staunch bourgeois nature derived directly from his family background.

While Degas remained aloof from the common public throughout his life, his attitude toward the "lower" professions was not due to any lack of sensitivity or warmth on his part, but a direct consequence of his upbringing. Although he himself was a man of moderate behavior, somewhat retiring and naturally elegant, he was indulgent toward the bohemian lifestyles of those around him. However, he tended to keep a distance from people of lower social standing: *"He agreed with the hierarchical and mundane vision of things reintroduced by the liberal bourgeoisie, which [under Louis Philippe] had taken*

the place of the political immigrants turfed out by the July Revolution. The caste spirit had been supplanted by the class spirit. The change was effected by the heroes of the trois glorieuses, *in the name of equality. The distances between social levels were unaffected[2]".*

And yet Degas' conventional attitudes were not only the product of his bourgeois education. His terse sayings, open criticisms and courageous stance on certain affairs, especially on politics, are distinctly his own.

He knew how to express himself, without modifying his ideas. He would have surely been a caricaturist if he had not fused his art with the grandeur of the past. His pictorial strictness afforded him no social deviation or tendency to paint caricatures – for criticism he preferred his verbal repartees, for which he became renowned and even feared. He was not unaware of the effect of his statements, which were often spoken in peremptory tones and contained a degree of paradox. His sallies in fact earned him enemies, especially in the art world, where he was branded as a muddled bourgeois.

His incisive ways gave him a reputation of cruelty, but instead of mitigating opinion, he often merely emphasized his point further. He was a nervous character, capricious even, and inevitably a victim of his own temper. As time progressed, Degas devoted more and more of his life to his art, which was completely immune from these traits.

In his old age, his personal isolation increased. He would certainly have fallen prey to insanity if his painting had been merely an outlet (as it was for Van Gogh) and not a means of achieving supreme harmony, a harmony that vested life with meaning, despite its many paradoxes. Without this world of inquiry, which became increasingly anguished toward the end (even pathetic in its prudery), Degas would have been just another bloated *pompier* or official artist. Furthermore, he had all the basic characteristics for becoming just that, and with his lack of

adventurousness he may well have overlooked the greater experiences of the spirit altogether.

But something was destined to happen that would change the mediocre painter (but gifted technician) into a superb artist, utterly freed from his rigid personal principles and rigid education.

His father, Pierre-Auguste-Hyacinthe arrived in Paris from Naples on the request of the founder of the dynasty, René Hilaire, a native of Orléans (1770) who had fled the 1789 Revolution and landed in Naples, where he had married and set up a bank. His son Pierre-Auguste was entrusted with the Paris branch in Rue de la Tour des Dames.

Once settled in Paris, Pierre-Auguste met a young creole woman from New Orleans, Célestine Musson, whom he married on July 12, 1832. Their son Edgar was born on July 19, 1834 at No. 8, Rue Saint Georges.

Over the following years, the family grew, and Célestine gave birth to Achille, who became an officer in the navy and René, who occupied himself with the affairs of the Musson family. Two daughters were born, one married an architect, the other a banker. The Degas household transferred first to No. 241, Rue Saint Honoré and then to No. 24, Rue de l'Ouest (today Rue d'Assas) and finally to Rue Madame, where Degas' mother passed away. In his biography, Jean Bouret cites the house as No. 26, Rue Madame (*Degas*, Somogy publishers), and P.A. Lemoisnes as No. 37. Degas' mother is mentioned little in the literature on the painter. In a small volume on Degas' youth, Jean-Marie Lhote writes: *Very little is ever said of Degas' mother. I was shocked to read on Degas' birth certificate how young his mother was. When he was born, his mother was nineteen, his father twenty-six. She was therefore wed at seventeen, which must have made her feel very close to her children. And it therefore surprises me that his biographers have overlooked her completely. I then realized that Lemoisne alluded to her on a couple of occasions, saying that Degas' father was widowed in 1847, or that the family lived* in Rue Madame, where the mother died. That was all.

But I only fully grasped what this meant when I saw the certificate attesting to her death on September 4, 1847, in No. 37, Rue Madame. "Marie Célestine Musson, aged thirty-two, born in New Orleans, wife of Degas, banker."

After giving birth to seven children (two of whom did not survive) this woman disappeared, when the painter was thirteen years old, and when the last-born, René, was merely two. We are not told whether she died while giving birth to an eighth child or from other causes. It is supposedly unimportant. But what was the effect of her death on the family life of the young Degas? Who raised the children? How did the future artist react? It is a mystery. This sheds some light on that utterly private world of feelings in which Degas was to close himself.

Jean-Marie Lhote quotes some of the many notes Daniel Halévy left regarding his friendship with the Degas family: The death of Degas' mother came in 1847. Degas was only thirteen years old when he lost her. He was inevitably deeply affected and I have tried to find traces of this painful blow. I was struck by the great sympathy Degas displayed toward Bartholomé on the death of the latter's wife in 1855. In my book I pointed out this great reservoir of feeling, but had never looked for its causes in the past experience of Degas himself. Now the causes are self-evident. Not only did Degas suffer a dire shock, but he witnessed the terrible grief of his father.

According to Halévy, the event had a decisive role in the formation of the child's character: I know this man well through my mother. My mother was a close friend of the Degas family, particularly of Degas' sister Marguerite, whom he loved dearly. It was Marguerite who explained the inner workings of the man. She said he would often sit at the piano, his hands slowly teasing out melodies from the keys. Music and art were the two enduring passions of his life.

Degas pére was a great connoisseur and sur-rounded himself with a cultured, wealthy class of people. While still a boy, Degas was able to frequent cultured, erudite people and collectors like Lacaze and Marcille. Marcille lived in Rue Monsieur le Prince in a small apartment packed with prized works of art which captivated the boy's imagination. To complete his education, Degas' father took him frequently to the city's museums. In fact, Edgar Degas was the most learned of his generation of painters and this early exposure influenced his absolute control of the medium. He copied many masterworks in the Louvre collection. One day, his contemporary Edouard Manet witnessed him skillfully etching a piece of copper to imitate a work by Velasquez. Amazed at such dexterity, Manet approached the young artist and they embarked on a close, tumultuous friendship that was enhanced by the similarity of their background, their common cultural makeup and bourgeois origins.

In another important household, at the home of the Valpinçon family, who were to play a vital role in Degas' life, the young artist first came into contact with the work of Ingres through a set of his drawings, including Odalisque with Turban, which fired his imagination for a long time. Thanks to his father, Degas met an eccentric collector by the name of Gregorio Soutzo, who taught him the rudiments of engraving. Edgar was in the meantime following the courses of Louis le Grand, whose other pupils Armand Deprez, Louis Bréguet (whose sister would marry Halévy), Arthur Desjardin and Henri Rouart would become Degas' longstanding friends.

Degas was not a model pupil however and had to settle for an honorable mention. Hence he shifted his attention to drawing. Where in most families an interest in drawing was considered a mere pastime, father Degas considered it something well worth encouraging in his son. On the death of his wife, Monsieur Degas moved to No. 4, Rue Mondovi where he gave his son the chance to set up a studio.

The windows of the house overlooked the Place de la Concorde and the Tuileries Gardens. As yet,

At any event, Degas *père* advised his son to put his name down for the Faculty of Law, which he duly did on November 12, 1853. But he soon tired of his studies at the university and cut his term short in order to better devote his time to his artistic education. At this point, it was essential to find a new teacher. A certain Louis Lamothe, recently arrived from Lyons with the Flandrin brothers, was chosen for the job. Lamothe had studied under Ingres but despite his superior talents he was overshadowed by his two friends. In an attempt to console him, Ingres had told him that upon his death he, Lamothe, would be his heir. It was Ingres also who advised Degas *père* through the Valpinçon family to put his son in Lamothe's care.

Thus it was through Lamothe that Degas would imbibe the work and theories of his revered master Ingres.

His studies led Degas to grasp that he should aim to capture the whole rather than the detail, to convey an attitude, a movement. In a kind of prophecy of the coming technology of photography, Ingres had said that an artist should be able to draw a man "falling from a roof," a message that was to have inestimable importance for Degas.

Another idea from the mind of Ingres was that the artist should preserve his individuality, though without overlooking the masters, copying their works with passion so as to acquire greater skill and assimilate pictorial tradition. This too was to find fertile ground in the young painter's mind and, of all his contemporaries, Degas was the only one not to reject the past and put tradition before revolution. Though he was closely linked to Impressionism, Degas' art remained somewhat isolated from that of his generation, providing a "classic" form of its own.

Unlike the true Impressionists, Degas scorned the *plein air* technique and claimed the right to draw straight from his imagination. While he was a keen observer of reality, when he chose his outside subjects he preferred to make preparatory sketches in his studio beforehand.

he had produced nothing, but with the moral support of his father he felt he was already a painter in his own right. When he received his diploma in letters in 1833, Edgar decided to try an academy and that year found a place as a "pupil of Barrias" at the Cabinet des Estampes (at the time directed by the painter Deveria) where his job was to copy the work of past masters.

At the time, engraving was the only means for reproducing these works. From his notes and sketches, we can see that Degas was particularly fond of Mantegna, Durer, Goya and Rembrandt. In order to deepen their acquaintance with the paintings they were copying, the students visited the Louvre often.

It was here rather than in the studio under Barrias that Degas acquired his unerring technique. Barrias was a painter of mediocre talents though a capable technician who, like many of his contemporaries, devoted his time to painting historical scenes. The public was avid for scenes of popular historical events and elaborate reworkings of history. Degas also went along with this trend, though the material was hardly suited to his ambitions and talents. He was not to remain long with Barrias, much to the anguish of his father.

From Degas' sketchbook
(photos courtesy Bibliothèque Nationale, Paris)

He was against improvisation and spontaneity, which he came across later, preferring a more premeditated, analytical approach.

But a fundamental difference was to distance the work of Degas from that of his predecessor Ingres. Ingres sustained that a well-drawn figure was subsequently a well-painted one. Degas was keen to find a warm and harmonious palette to suit his intentions and decided to imitate Veronese's vibrant use of color. But this did not mean he was not observant of the reality about him. In his bedroom-studio in Rue Mondovi he entertained family members and friends. With the utmost care he reproduced the lineaments of his sister Thérèse and his brother René. His portrait of Marguerite was sanguine, without ignoring the delicate Florentine traits he was so fond of.

On occasion, he took courage and handled the canvas in a different way, as in the portrait of his grandfather Germain Musson. In absence of models to paint, Degas frequently did self-portraits, which provide us with a rich range of images of the painter throughout the period. One of Degas' first biographers sketches the artist's appearance: *Degas was rather short with a strong head, a mischievous look, high domed forehead, chestnut-colored silky hair, a quick cunning eye and arched eyebrows in the form of a circumflex; his nose slightly turned up, wide nostrils, thin mouth half-hidden beneath a scanty beard that was never trimmed.*

On the insistence of Lamothe, in 1855 Degas joined the Ecole des Beaux Arts. There is little trace of his passage through the Ecole, perhaps because he frequented the courses rather sporadically. The diligent copying of plaster models (because live models were a rarity) and the methodical nature of the teaching had disgusted him. By now he was working from originals to compensate for the antiquated and jaded scholastic system. He turned down the chance to stay at the Villa Medici in Rome because he hoped to be able to travel privately through Italy some time, given the economic well-being of his family. This he managed to do. At school he made friends with Fantin-Latour, Tourny and Bonnat. The last two were to rendezvous with him in Italy in 1857 and 1858. But apart from the sessions at school and his intense painting work, Degas' life was rather uneventful. In this aura of work and diligence, the young artist's character gradually took shape. He was discreet, hard-working, aloof, keen on maintaining his independence, selfish and sickly. Degas' work betrays a deep problem that his biographers take pains to ignore but which was clearly decisive throughout his life. This reserved, orderly, meticulous life seemed to conceal an enduring but wholly personal drama.

Was this great purist a troubled soul? Andrè Gide once noted that "if we look closely at any moral reform, we can always find a physiological mystery, a dissatisfaction of the flesh, some profound disturbance or anomaly".

As for his morals, he stood out even in his youth. A rather critical Gustave Coquiot commented that Degas was easily moody, a melancholy sort who would not brook vulgarity. "The impression he makes is of a young man who keeps constant control over himself," wrote Coquiot. "He kept these refined manners all his life. He was precise, severe, dry, had a horror of movement, of agitation and uncontrolled passion. He was a sullen notary, erratic, bizarre, almost misanthropic."

There are very few surviving works from this formative period. The first recorded works date from when he was nineteen to twenty-five years old, though there is little of distinction.

It was not until 1860 that Degas began to paint with inspiration and a more evolved technique, as in *The Belleli Family*, *Young Spartans* and *Jophé's Daughter*. The only painting that shows any signs of disturbance is *The Belleli Family*. These signs were to increase after the death of his father in February 1874, whose unceasing comments and opinions had always been a tremendous influence on the youth.

It is interesting to note that Degas as an innovator

26

only emerged after the death of the one person he had always tried not to contradict. Jean-Marie Lhote has commented that the problem afflicting Degas the artist was his astonishing lack of talent at the start of his career. His sketches are clumsy, and yet he can copy masterworks with great perception or build up a portrait with a fair amount of skill. Even in the most important works, with their apparent light-hearted touches and furtive strokes, we can detect a timid man. It may well be that this was the characteristic that determined his behavior in the outside world.

(1) Georges Rivière. *Degas*. Floury.
(2) Special issue of the magazine *Bizarre*.

A PILGRIMAGE TO ITALY

Up until the 19th century it was considered almost essential for artists to travel to Italy to acquire a proper understanding of technique, especially since the traditional system of apprenticeship had gradually fallen into disuse. Degas, however, put off such a journey, deciding that his first priority was to find a method and a form of expression of his own beforehand. What was later to become an obsession had begun to show in his early youth and justified his later travels through Italy. From the very start Degas strove to dominate a technique that was still only inchoate. During this period, *the copies he made of the works of the great masters of the past do not seem to be solely aimed at improving his drawing and composition skills or his style, but at acquiring the basic skills that he felt were lacking in the work of contemporary artists and of their immediate predecessors[1].*

For this reason, going to Italy was a way of returning to the very origins of his art. The social standing of the Degas family and the presence of relatives resident in Italy made the journey a more viable proposal. In 1854 Degas went to stay at his uncle's in Naples and the sheer spectacle of the landscape reawakened his senses: *On the way out of Civitavecchia the sea is clear blue; at midday it becomes apple-green with streaks of indigo on the horizon, where a row of small sailboats resemble a flock of gulls... the sea was stirring slightly and turned a light green-gray, with silver crests and a vapory horizon blending with the gray sky. The Castel dell'Ovo rose up like a golden outcrop. The boats on the sand were like patches of sepia. But this was not the cold gray of the Channel. It was more like the downy gray throat of a pigeon.*

These unemotional and unembellished notes enable us to identify the place with precision. In certain rare landscapes, Degas preferred a more immediate impression based, however, on an exact knowledge of the objects before him. Besides the natural surroundings, which particularly fired his imagination (and he was rarely as eloquent about his findings as he was here), Degas found many examples of art on which he wished to work. He left a list of paintings that caught his attention. *La vergine dalla lunga gamba* by Giulio Romano, Titian's *Pope Paul III*, a *Saint Catherine* by Correggio, a *Pope Leo X* by Andrea del Sarto and finally, rather incongruously, a painting by Claude Lorrain which Degas described as being the "most beautiful one could ever see, the sky is silver and the trees speak."

He by no means disdained ancient art and considered it "the most powerful art form and the most enchanting." Perhaps out of an excess of prudery, Degas makes no attempt to describe what he saw of Naples. And yet in no other era was Naples more enjoyable, more fabulous and more "corrupt". Was there really nothing for this rather stiff young man to delight in?

Gustave Coquiot declares his amazement: *At the time, 1856, neither the "salvation army" nor the scandal had managed to curb the rampant prostitution of this filthy city, in which sex was flaunted in broad daylight.*

In a letter to his mother dated 1851, Gustave Flaubert tactfully censors his observations: *My stay in Naples was utterly delightful. The women are brazen in attitude and ride in open carriages hatless, with flowers in their hair. But it is the air that does it. In Chiaia (which is a grand chestnut-lined esplanade on the waterfront with a pergola-like tunnel of greenery and the sound of lapping waves) the flower-girls push their violets straight into your button-hole. You have to be stern with them to keep yourself from being molested.*

On similar lines, Louis Bouilhet was also impressed: *Naples is so appealing because of the great quantity of women that abound here. There is a whole quarter of town filled with prostitutes standing on their front doorsteps. This is the original Suburra. As you walk down the street they pull their skirts up above their heads to show you their c... and then ask for some money. They even follow you in* this position. *This was the most incredible thing I had ever seen by way of prostitution and cynicism. Even the sun is in love. Everything is so gay and easy. The horses are adorned with peacock feathers behind their ears.*

But the excitement and exoticism of Naples seems to have left Degas indifferent and he preferred to go about his cultural itinerary. The truculent Gustave Coquiot draws his own somewhat hasty conclusions on Degas' behavior: *They told him to be a wise and disciplined pupil and copy the works of the great masters. And such he became, unable to see nature if not through their interpretations. The blood in his veins had thus been transfused once, twice, three times and he was to remain marked by this operation for all his life.*

In 1855 Degas entered the Beaux-Arts and made a second journey to Italy the following year, stopping in Rome where he met Tourny and painted his portrait.

He spent 1857 in Florence at the home of his aunt Belleli, completing numerous portraits and sketches of family members.

On this journey Degas made some very interesting notes: *Rome to Florence, July 24, 1858. Left Rome at 6:45 am. Reached a high spot near Ponte Molle, a superb plain, a dream-like Italy. Yellow plains with mown wheat, gray hillside as the night falls at the foot of the mountains. Hazy, more vaporous than blue exactly, black and lacking the different planes of the mountainside. Seven thirty. Except for the yellow foreground, everything is gray. I can make out the volcanic areas, stony patches with clumps of trees.*

Capranica. Uphill, downhill. I was amazed entering Viterbo, it resembled Avignon so much. Cathedral only memories – ruins to the left and right – beneath the little archway, what a fine view of the city!

Italian silence, typical of Papal cities (which is really sleepiness). I return on the Angelus. Go back out at five. It's Sunday – every curve in the road, gothic porticoes. Porta San Martino – it's like Provence. Chiesa della Verità, superb frescoes by Lorenzo da Viterbo. At the left transept, a fresco of the Virgin Mary. Traces of paint on the walls. Angels holding up a curtain. The church ceiling is shaped like a basilica and the roof has square tiles – typically Italian, enchanting taste. I go back to the chapel designed by Lorenzo da Viterbo, it is superb with its charming heads. I follow the bastions toward a Paradiso by Sebastiano del Piombo. The resemblance to Avignon is incredible. Ten in the evening. I leave for Orvieto, in the moonlight. I can make out the mountains and the landscape. Superb countryside. Montefiascone. Mountains. It is dawn, mist in the plains. We descend the valley at Orvieto. The cathedral pokes out above the mist. I climb the steps, an eagle's nest, white eagles. The cathedral is sublime, I am enraptured. A rich façade, doubtful taste. Recent mosaics from a decadent period. I recognize some of the sculptures: I go in and rush to the works of Luca Signorelli. In the more beautiful monuments there is this mixture of styles. I recognized the beauty of the famous seraphs. I am speechless: it is such a dream I can scarcely remember... subjects from Dante, ingenious, palpitating. Arabesques, almost angry, contrast of love and movement by Luca Signorelli, with the peace of the blessed Angel, especially Christ, as beautiful as ever. The style is Michelangelo. I tour the church and then go back to the hotel as I am dog-tired. Sleep till noon, have lunch then write to Uncle Achille. I visit the well at San Patrizio. A superb view from the fortress, with the Tiber at the valley bottom. I go to the cathedral and begin drawing one of the seraphs. The organist plays from the Traviata, such derision. I take a walk along the bastions, along the streets amidst the medieval houses. The sun is behind Monte Cimio. I feel no urge to draw the landscape.

I am thrilled by Luca Signorelli. I have to study the vaulted ceiling against the background. Toward seven o'clock I walk up to the citadel. Near the wells I take in the plains, a superb sight to remember all one's life. The sun sets. Toward the road to Florence, all the various surfaces of the mountainside. The finest monument of the day. I think of France, which is not as beautiful.

But my love for home and for my work in a small corner override this desire to enjoy the sight of such splendid scenery. Everything changes, night has arrived.

In this silence, one can hear the slightest noise.

After a sleepless night I slept through the morning.

Midday, conversation with the family in the next room. The young lady is in the care of a rather grubby Parisian. San Domenico, small piazza, tranquil, charming tombs, but unfortunately it is almost nightfall. The weather turns bad, a storm is brewing, sadness in the soul, the bastions built for the sunshine have taken a leaden color from the sky. There are beautiful women and girls. They have the grace of the Florentines without the wildness of the Roman women. Dinner. The boredom of leavetaking. Departure to Perugia in the rain and lightning. We are in the mountains, uphill, downhill, moonlight. July 29. I reach the hilltop town of Civita della Pieve at 5:30 am. It is set in plains surrounded by mountains crowned by white clouds. In the cathedral a fine Perugino on the altar, very fine painting (representing Saint Paul of Lyons?) of considerable size. Church outside the town wall, fine painting on right as you go in, perhaps of the French school. Looks like the Neapolitan countryside, as the land is fertile and well-cultivated. I go back to the hotel, I am tired and not knowing what to do I write to Rouget. At 4:30 I walk toward the lake, Lake Chiusi. Storms on the horizon. Traveling alone you go through towns filled with works of art. I am tired of contemplating nature. Priests on foot everywhere. The women resemble those in Perugino's paintings. Is this just my imagination?

Ten in the evening: Departure for Perugia. There

are six of us. We reach Perugia at quarter to four, towed up the hill into Perugia by a pair of oxen. The effect is magnificent, two rows of pilgrims crossing the street in front of the Governor's residence, singing and waiting on the steps of the Cathedral. It is barely daylight, I can just glimpse the faces of some of those sitting on the cathedral steps. The old building is very tall. You have to look upward to get an idea of the space that surrounds us.

Hotel della Corona. At 8:30 am I rush off: the cathedral is full of pilgrims who make a general buzzing noise. Perugia is an imposing place, everything is new to me. The Cathedral has been badly restored inside. Unrecognizable. A Descent from the Cross by Romano, the best seen yet. Vast talent but nothing that moves me. A Virgin with Child by Luca Signorelli, a San Lorenzo, a saint with a planet. Superb colors, resembles the one in San Giovanni in Laterano. Rain, heavy storm, I wander about. I get as far as Monte Luce, superb view across the valley, not as uneven as the one toward Rome. San Domenico is completely disfigured, a superb portal. In the church they are repairing the window on the Choir, a chapel on left, a Beato Angelico. Another Beato Angelico in the sacristy, part of a tabernacle with three angels of the Annunciation.

The Collegio dei Cangi (in Cambio). I knew the composition, but the colors! It is Perugino's finest work. Gianicolo Chapel, fine colors. The Libyan and Eritrean Sibyls are larger than usual, like those done by Raphael. The little chapel is harmony itself. Perugino self-portrait, 1453.

Palazzo Connestabili. A most adorable Virgin by Raphael, such fine brushwork, the child's arm is a marvel.

San Pietro fuori le Mura (San Pietro dei Cassinensi), in the Sacristy a head of Christ, five figures by Perugino. In San Benedetto a magnificent copy of a Raphael in the style of Perugino. The sky has turned dark, the church is too dark to see any more. I must not forget the effect of the clouds glimpsed between Porta Carmine and Porta Sole as they threw a shadow across the plains and the mountain of Assisi was still in full sunlight.

Saturday, July 31. The weather is changeable. At seven I set off on foot and by ten I am at Santa Maria degli Angeli. Full of pilgrims, large church. The organ was playing during the mass, the interplay of human voices was superb. I am not religious in the normal sense, but I was deeply moved, the fine music moved me more than the pilgrims who beat their chests, full of faith. The fresco by Overbeck is fine, but is not worth too much research.

The climb to Assisi drained me of whatever energies I had left. It is all steps. My pleasure at seeing the church set me right: twelve miles on foot would be plenty even for someone stronger than myself. I finally find the Cosanelli inn mentioned in my guide, and rest but I am quite exhausted. I caught the sun in my face and have a headache, I suppose it is nothing. San Francesco, the upper church is a proper church with stained-glass windows. Sublime episodes from the life of Saint Francis – as soon as I get back to Paris I must go to the Bibliothèque... I have not time to stop long, and fear I may have a dizzy spell. The lower church reminds me of the little picture by Granet. I stand where the artist worked, the sun through the central window blinds me. I feel regret at seeing so many fine things. I have to go. Everything reeks of prayer. Everything is beautiful, the details, the whole, I prefer not to try anything rather than risk a mere sketch, without having carefully studied everything first. My memories of it all should be enough. Giotto has great expression and drama, he is a genius. I have seen some extraordinary sights indeed. The peasants began to run, singing and shouting the names of the patron saints around the altar, following a curious rite of devotion. They kept it up with great energy like Dervishes. Perhaps it could explain the Crusades. I heard a friar speaking French and went closer. We spoke. He is from Paris.

He led me up to the terrace from where you can see as far as Spello. He was previously a man of the world, a charming person. He seems to feel sorrow for those still out there. Tomorrow morning he is to become a sub-deacon.

I will go to Sant'Apollinare. He led me to his cell and we spoke at great length. For midday I am off to Santa Filomena.

Sunday morning. Giotto: sublime movement in Saint Francis chasing out the demons. Saint Francis talks with Christ. I have never been so moved, I wept, I shall not stay. At eight at the church of Sant'Apollinare where father Pascal was to be ordained sub-deacon. I was moved to tears. How many thoughts went through my mind, and who knows if these things will come to pass. The choirboys were dressed in black with a white surplice and cape round their shoulders. I should have plucked up courage and done some sketches. If I had been fifty without children or a bachelor I might well have stopped here, perhaps in a monastery.

Entering from the left in the upper church two figures of saints on the cornice, like the paintings in Pompei, pious figures, but what fine shapes. The choir stall bears heads of Franciscan monks carved into the wooden facing. I go down, crying. These were people who felt life to the full and in truth renounced nothing. They knew what it meant to toil. If I too could only know, if only my character could be such to produce paintings that were as valid as these sermons. I am not a religious painter, I cannot feel what they feel, and my praying seems to be prompted by my emotions alone. After I had been in the church over three and half hours I went to see father Pascal, who was resting in his cell, to try and get over the rush of emotion of this morning. We talked for a long time. I can remember the conversation but shall not record it here.

What indecision. I must leave Assisi, sending my luggage on to Florence by coach. But I am afraid of falling prey to fantasies, which may one day be useful, but which prevent me from working. I think I heard Rivière pronounce father Pascal's name when he was reading the act of ordainment. He takes me to the Englishman whose wife I had met the previous evening in church and that morning during the ordainment. His French is good, he was a pupil of Delaroche. I tell him I want to come back here, that I love Assisi. By seven I am at the church of the Angeli. I find a carriage bound for San Paolo. Some beautiful girls on a cart ahead of us, one of whom is my coachman's girl. His horse cannot proceed to San Giovanni and he leaves me with a suspicious looking lad. It is night already, but there is little point in being afraid. We reach our destination. That girl that climbed in between the coachman and myself... I wanted to return to Assisi. I was fantasizing so much over this idea that I discussed fares. Fifty lire to go back to Assisi tomorrow morning.

Monday morning, five thirty. I have the bags taken out to the carriage. I am just about to leave: I am undecided. Then I stay. I stop three asses to go to Arezzo via Cortona and leave at eight. First I pass by the convent San Severo to see the frescoes by Raphael and Fra Bartolomeo. My thoughts are with Assisi, it draws me like a lover. I want to leave, however. The sacristy has a very fine work by Pisanello. Perugino seems the same. In front of the hotel I see Clère and Delaunay and greet them. Heated discussion with two carriage drivers, a difficult lot. Wednesday we will go to Arezzo, tomorrow to Assisi. I am very pleased about this. I will be able to see father Pascal. Assisi is so attractive, the very reason I must flee it. Its church filled me with emotion, I adore its painters, those plains and those mountains which emanate love, happiness, where perhaps I too shall be happy one day. I am impatient. On the way up the Angeli hillside road with its cypresses and tunnels. I am not so enthusiastic about the picturesqueness of Italy – what is so moving is the eternal style! The Englishman and his wife (I was glad to see them again) are intimately happy. I too will find a simple, calm woman who can understand my spiritual self and with whom I can spend my days modestly pursuing my work.

Is this not a wonderful dream? I'm about to return to Paris: who knows what will become of me. I will always be an honest man. I hope my memory will allow me to complete what I have written, which is only a small part of what I have been thinking. I have abandoned any idea of sketching.

What was supposed to be a short stay in Florence turned out to be a long sojourn, as Degas' aunt had to stay at her ailing father's bedside in Naples. Degas was thus able to admire the many treasures of the city and follow the advice contained in his father's letters. *The masters of the 15th century are your true guides. Once you have fully absorbed their lesson and you have unceasingly perfected your pictorial skills through diligent study, then you will achieve results. Although some point out imperfections, they are the masters of the masters and one must become an enthusiast of their works.*

Degas' stay in Florence was prolonged even further by the absence of his Aunt Belleli and the death of grandfather Hyacinthe. Edgar worked intensely and with great determination. Upon receiving his work, Degas' father wrote: *I am most satisfied and can tell you that you have made a great step forward in your art. Your drawing hand is confident and the color tones correct. You have rid yourself of the limp style of Flandrin and Lamothe and of that gray, earthen color... Rest assured my dear Edgar, you are on the right road. Proceed with a calm spirit, work steadily and follow the path you have marked out for yourself. This is your path, and yours alone. Work calmly and keep to this path and you will certainly achieve greatness. You have an admirable future, do not be discouraged, do not worry.*

Victim of a common prejudice for portrait painting, Degas *père* notes: *You say you are bored with painting portraits. You must try to overcome it because this will be the most prized jewel in your crown.*

In fact, upon his return to Florence, Degas set about composing his series of portraits of the famous Belleli family.

First he produced a great many sketches and drawings, and then embarked on the composition itself. In Paris, his father was anxious that he did not abuse the hospitality of his brother-in-law. He entreated the youth to return to Paris, once more giving his advice: *You have studied the work of the 15th-century fresco painters, you have soaked your spirit in them, you have completed drawings and watercolors after their work to record the colors of their palette. You have analyzed the fantastic tones and marvelous drawing skills of Giorgione, but have you assimilated his genius?*

We can assume that all this advice was devoutly followed by the young artist. In a later letter, his father declares: *I am pleased you have closely studied Giorgione; though realistic, the tone of his colors needs more warmth. Be careful of dark tones: this is a mistake of those who want warm tones but cannot or will not see when they copy the Venetian masters and reproduce the colors from nature. It is essential to discover and capture the devices of these masters without falling prey to constrictions: when you are faced with nature, you must use your inspiration.*

When Degas returned to Paris, his portrait of the Belleli family was probably unfinished. He completed it in the winter of 1859, interrupted by brief visits to Italy.

Although the portrait started out as a classic representation of people in a family environment, Degas arranged the subjects in a markedly innovative manner, with the emphasis on realism, creating an almost photographic exactness. However, the people portrayed do not seem to be posing, but are caught in the intimacy of family intercourse. To a greater degree than his contemporaries, Degas was most receptive to the style that became Duranty's hallmark. And like Edouard Manet and Henri Toulouse-Lautrec (whom he was to influence strongly), Degas watched as the society entered the new age.

Semiramis, Building Babylon. (1861)
Paris, Louvre.
This is not far from J. P. Laurens, but it is better.

Unlike Manet, who painted instinctively and was boldly driven by a sensual temperament, Degas was so conscientious of the notions instilled in him that his progress was painfully slow, burdened by his technical preparation that made him indecisive and enduringly dissatisfied. While Degas himself devised some new and bold ideas, he withdrew into a world of strictly technical problems.

Just as Impressionism was making its mark, championed by Edouard Manet, Degas seemed almost reactionary.

(1) Denis Rouart. *Degas à la recherche de sa technique.* Floury.

A DIFFICULT BEGINNING

In most painters, a success of this kind would have signaled the start of a series of pictures in the same vein, a burst of progress. But this was not so for Degas. His scrupulousness virtually suffocated every impulse, every spark of instinct and experiment. Degas began to paint the kind of compositions and tours de force that his contemporaries produced in order to be accepted by the Salon.

Like Manet, Degas was torn between his reverence for the past and his visions of the future. While Manet was desperately trying to improve his social status and sought some official consecration, such as participating in a Salon or some kind of decoration, Degas threw himself into painting historical scenarios, searching for a kind of painting genre that would need no external justification.

This ambition led to the painting *Young Spartans*, which shows the painter in a moment of transition. Although his conception of art was itself classical, Degas was spurned by the Classicists owing to the accentuated realism of his canvases. They found him too dry, too intellectual. Whether they were right or wrong, Degas was simply demonstrating his technical abilities. In the meantime, a new concept was just emerging, a new lead that Jean-Baptiste-Camille Corot had begun to follow that would soon blossom in Impressionism.

He continued his series of portraits, which included his sister Marguerite, Madame Hertel, the Valpinçons, Ruelle (the cashier at his father's bank) and, when there was no one else to paint, Degas did self-portraits.

Degas' talent is actually clearer to see in these portraits than in the more academic works like *Young Spartans*. His talent was only just forming. The portrait of his friend Léon Bonnat testifies to his progress. It was painted in 1862-63 and shows a masterly handling of color, lucid tones and a reigning calm, embodying a realist style that was suggested to Degas by one of his most esteemed friends. Rather than idealizing his model, Degas tried to capture his essential physical character:

The Belleli Family. (detail).

The Belleli Family. (1860)
Paris, Louvre.
A group portrait that is also a social document: the picture of a class
attentive to order and dignity, in the artist's own image.

Why shouldn't we depict some of the ugliness that surrounds us all the time instead of systematically reproducing beauty? What is most beautiful is the physical character, the play of light on the person's features, the structure of the face, the life that flows just beneath the skin[1].

Degas was far more ruthless than Manet in this respect. Critic Germain Bazin commented that Degas was "a kind of bourgeois version of Saint Simon".

Still prey to his obsessions, Degas returned to Paris and devoted himself to painting historical scenes, rather than allow himself to be steered toward the kind of subject most suited to his genius.

Unfortunately, the historical genre was already extinct. "Historical painting", opined Théophile Gautier, "is being eclipsed day by day, together with everything that has nothing to do with everyday reality". It was somewhat utopian of Degas to imagine combining his love for ancient art, classical rules and undisputed technical mastery, with a love for contemporary life and the realist urge found in Manet's work. In the same year, Manet painted some of his most well-known works: *Musiques aux Tuileries, The Spanish Singer, Lola of Valencia* and *Déjeuner sur l'herbe.*

It must be said that, given his cultural background, Degas was more suited than others of his generation to this "historical" genre. His sketchbooks of 1860 and 1865 contain a great many projects, five of which were actually carried through.

Degas was fully aware of the novelty of his subjects. P. A. Lemoisne had this to say: *He attempts to imbue his characters with ease and naturalness as if they were about to carry out normal everyday activities. While he does not clothe them in modern dress, he avoids indulging in the kind of archaeological decoration so dear to his contemporaries. By generalizing the type of figure and simplifying the accessories, he tries to animate the scene by concentrating on the action and the character of the figures[2].*

In addition to the Spartan figures mentioned above, other paintings from this particular period include *Semiramis Building Babylon* and *Alexander and Bucephalus.*

The first of the two contains some fine execution, such as the secondary figure of a maiden-in-waiting inserted in the foreground. The canvas is generally imbued with a warm, golden and even sensual feeling. But the most important of the entire series is the canvas *Misadventures of the City of Orléans (Medieval War Scenes)*, a subject that gave Degas a pretext to paint a series of fine nudes, at the suggestion of Ingres. Although in this painting Degas did not actually manage to capture the principles inherent to this particular genre, the work confirmed the artistic features the artist would continue to try out with more appropriate subjects.

The real beginning of Degas as a painter was 1865-1870, during which he executed fifty or more portraits, at first single figures and then groups, which would eventually make him a keen chronicler of the evolving society around him. In one of his notebooks he set down the guidelines for his research: *Do a study of modern feeling as the first expression (academic style); study del Sarto's observations on passionate movement of the eye; beauty ought to be a certain kind of physiognomy; the mystery of the Belle Ferronnière is not her state of repose, but her lack of expression; remember the ivory-pink color of women in green or black velvet dresses, just like the primitives used to do...*

None of those portraits was executed without some deep-felt need, a strong sense of curiosity for the model in question and an enthusiastic understanding of the model's mind, as none of them was actually commissioned as such.

This was not the case with Pierre Auguste Renoir, whose portraits provided his daily bread.

Degas picked his models from his normal surroundings and rather than have them pose, he would study their lineaments and proceed not by painting immediately what he saw, but what his keen eye recalled. Little by little, Degas passed from the portrait to the larger composition, in which the artist's interest shifts from the face to the clothing and hands and thence to the gestures of his subjects. He was keen to capture people in their daily attitudes and above all strove to lend a unity of expression to the body and face. The figure was set in a situation that underlined his or her character. He would make those people laugh for whom laughter was a typical gesture, capturing their most natural or recurring expression. By slotting his subjects into specific scenes he gradually had to become more aware of the layout and use props, create a scenario, as in the case of *Portrait of Madame Hertel (Lady with Chrysanthemums)*, in which the face is situated to one side to allow room for the fiery bunch of flowers, which almost steal the picture. At this point, Degas was once more worried about getting the light right: *Work over the effects of evening light, lamps, candles... It is vital to show not the light source but its effects. This aspect of art can become of immense importance and cannot be overlooked.*

While working on his portrait of Thérèse Morbilli, Degas made an important discovery, namely, pastels.

So far he had used this technique for quick sketching. Pastels had enabled him to capture expressions and glimpses of activity with great rapidity. When he first stumbled on the technique, Degas had no subject to try it out on. But later, when he discovered the corridors of the Opéra and the ballerinas, who became a recurring theme throughout his work, he systematically pursued his research into the effects of the new medium.

(1) P. A. Lemoisne.
(2) P. A. Lemoisne.

*Misadventures in the City of Orléans
(Medieval War Scenes).* (1865)
Paris, Louvre.
We have several preparatory sketches of this scene, the historical subject
of which is unknown.

Portrait of Thérèse Degas. (1863)
Paris, Louvre.
A sort of majesty, less conformist than "modern". She belies the
self-assurance of a class buttressed by its riches and its social power.

La Pédicure. (1873)
Paris, Louvre.
A sort of prelude to a long series of studies of "femmes à la toilette",
self-absorbed in their personal care.

THE CAFÉ GUERBOIS

No. 11, Rue Batignolles (today Avenue de Clichy) was the site of the Café Guerbois, the gathering point for all those who were directly or indirectly involved in the problems affecting the upcoming generation of artists who were struggling to overcome the intransigence of the previous generation, to erode the conformism of the era and to topple the academic stranglehold of the Institut.

At the center of these often rowdy get-togethers was Edouard Manet. The regulars included Astruc, Emile Zola, Duranty, Duret, Guillemet, Bracquemond and Bazille. But they were often accompanied by Fantin-Latour, Renoir, Degas and the photographer Nadar. Those who lived out of town, like Paul Cézanne, Alfred Sisley, Camille Pissarro and Claude Monet made it a point to stop by when passing through Paris. In his memoirs, Monet spoke enthusiastically of the Café Guerbois: *There was nothing more exciting than these discussions and the clash of opinions. They stimulated the mind, spurred new and sincere research. They restored your enthusiasm, leaving you energized for weeks on end until the definitive idea emerged. You came away from the meetings with fresh determination, your thinking clearer and more defined*[1].

The most important meetings were held on Thursday, when issues of aesthetics were discussed, together with the economic problems that plagued most of the artists.

Of the entire crowd, only Manet, Berthe Morisot and Degas himself were unaffected by financial worries. According to Manet, Degas was quite clearly lacking in understanding when he told Fantin-Latour that he could see little sense in an art that was within reach of the poorer classes, enabling them to "deliver pictures worth a mere thirteen sous". Degas was often contradictory and regularly insisted on praising works that were quite clearly lacking in talent.

He was a spirited debater but reasoned with an appalling lack of good sense and was quickly upset when the discussion revolved around political

allet of Robert the Devil. (1872)
ew York, Metropolitan Museum.
he expressiveness of this painting pivots on both the highly contrasted
ghting and a brushstroke with an extraordinarily modern vibrancy.

Lady with Chrysanthemums. (1865)
New York, Metropolitan Museum.
A very innovative perspective in the composition, similar to that in
Hortense Valpinçon (1869) and *Woman with Oriental Vase* (1872).

issues or drawing technique. *He would never give in, and would sometimes explode with rage, use harsh words and cut people off. Compared to him, Alceste was mild and weak*[2].

Another member of the group, Duranty, observed that Degas was an artist of rare intelligence who, unlike his colleagues, was deeply interested in ideas: *Since there was neither method nor transition in his mind, which was in constant ferment, he was dubbed the inventor of "social chiaro-scuro"*.

Indeed, Degas rejected theories on art. He would grumble that the Muses never debate among themselves: *At night fall, when their work is done, they dance and do not speak.*

Like Manet, Degas was always very well-groomed and often beguiled his listener with his immaculate dress and paradoxical manner. His fame as a cynic and impetuous type stems from his very first encounters with the group of young artists. This opinion was amplified when he was suspected of being a misanthrope to boot. John Rewald helps complete the profile of this strange man: *Alongside the others he looked almost frail and his features, gestures and speech had an aristocratic and even antiquated air, in stark contrast with the atmosphere of the café. Often he was alone in the defense of his ideas and preferences. But it was hard to tell where his seriousness ended and his irony began. It was difficult to stand against him in a discussion, not just because he seemed to have a great many arguments, but because he did not hesitate to reduce his adversaries to silence with aphorisms that were unanswerable, aphorisms that were frequently cutting or cruel, and always forcefully delivered.*

Manet and Degas were to some extent drawn to each other by their common background, frequently against others of more modest origins. Their opinions on modernity often had the same ring. Due to their education, culture and class prejudices, both perceived the same kind of problems. Nonetheless they often clashed and judged each other harshly. Degas fell out with his friend because

Manet had split Degas' portrait of him and his wife, as he felt that the latter half was not good enough. For his part, Manet told his sister-in-law Berthe Morisot that Degas lacked spontaneity, and could never love a woman.

Though fully aware of Degas' aversion for women, Ambroise Vollard was less severe in his judgment: *No one has loved women like Degas has, but a mixture of prudery and timidity kept him apart from them.*

In the Café Guerbois period, a terrible internal battle was going on between the old and the new Degas. *Here is an artist who is at first enthusiastic about the accepted masters, who believes in tradition, in the Institut. A serious-minded and wealthy young painter sets off for Rome to get his education. He falls in with all the members of the Academy he comes across. He forces himself to spend long hours in the museums; he ponders the words of Ingres: "draw and paint the works of the masters before approaching nature". He turns out rigid, classical portraits, gags himself. He copies whole paintings without omitting a single detail. He paints historical compositions. They say he nearly won the Prix de Rome, but through his unflagging efforts he will get into the Institut. In the end, he had become a hardworking, disciplined and esteemed painter, after having followed the masters, professor Lamothe and above all Ingres, this neo-Raphael will end his career bearing the award of Légion d'Honneur across his breast. All this is clear in his organized mind, because it is the logical conclusion to everything that has gone before. But one evening a little genie snoozing in his brain suddenly wakes up, and in the guise of Duranty, steers him toward the Café Guerbois, where he meets other painters. Young empassioned men with rousing arguments. "We have to burn all academic painting", they say, "destroy the Institut". Degas is dumbfounded, but Duranty explains to him that they are right and that the world is tired of insipid, conventional paintings; that they have to reject once and for all the Greek and Roman subjects, the Battle of Salamina and the defeat of Pompei; that the anachronisms of the old painters should be relegated to the hardware store; that it is essential to deal directly with nature, with the current day and age, with our own customs and paint new realistic canvases, living canvases. Will Degas be equal to this task? He set his mind to it. He spends every evening at the Café Guerbois, but once back in his studio he prays to Ingres. Degas has a split nature: he is both an academic and a modernist. He cannot decide which to follow. He then asks himself if perhaps this devotion to modern themes is not just an angry reaction, while his inner store of tradition, education and accepted opinion draw him, quite calmly, toward everything that is arid in the museums*[3].

Degas' leaning toward modernism finally got the upper hand and one day Duranty pronounced that Degas was about to become the painter of high society[4]. This was not so far from the truth, since his models always came straight from his own social circles while he steadily prepared his modern vision, his illustration of contemporary life.

In 1886 the de Goncourt brothers published *Manette Salomon*, in which one of the characters expressed ideas that Degas was to make his own: *Every age has its own idea of beauty, any kind of beauty, more or less basic, comprehensible and pliable... It is a question of investigation. Perhaps today beauty is hidden, concealed and concentrated... To find it we need analysis, a magnifying glass, myopic eyes, new physiological procedures. The question of modernity is considered vacuous and just a paradox of everyday truth to catch the public's attention: realism.*

A certain gentleman has founded a "chamber" religion of ugliness, beastliness and vulgarity, badly and indiscriminately put together; modernity, characterless, expressionless, lacking what is beautiful and the life of ugliness in nature and in art, style, [...] sensation, the intuition of the contemporary and the spectacle that passes close by, of the present in which you feel your passions and something your own.

Everything is there for the artist, the 19th century not to be painted. But it is inconceivable. A century that has suffered the great century of scientific disquiet and the anguish of truth. We must find a line to follow that will give us some idea of life, of the individual, uniqueness. Like a model *à la Houdon or a preparation à la La Tour,* a form *à la Gavarni. A kind of drawing more real than any other, a more human kind of drawing.*

These ideas are similar to those Degas reported in his notebook of 1859: *Paint all objects of everyday use so that they reflect the life of a man and woman, like a dresser's dummy that preserves the form of the body.*

Then Degas lists the subjects he would like to try out: *A series of musicians with their instruments, another series focused on bakers with still lifes with bread and cakes, a series on smoke (cigarettes, steam engines, chimneys, steamships). A series devoted to mourning (veils, gloves, undertakers), a series of ballerinas (with studies of their legs), a series of impressions of the Café in the evening under different lighting and reflections in the mirrors.*

Degas did in fact paint a great many of these subjects, but from the point of view of an usher, like some kind of inventory rather than as a pretext for plastic experimentation.

Paradoxically, Degas discovered pure painting just as he was going blind and approaching a form of realism that went beyond the momentary and the fortuitous, the accidental and the picturesque, to reach the universal. He was to become more modern when, contrary to the Impressionists, instead of trying to discover the changing aspects of nature, he sought that "living, human, intimate line" of the de Goncourts.

(1) Interview with Thiebault-Sisson, in *Le Temps,* November 27, 1900.
(2) Paul Valéry.
(3) Gustave Coquiot.
(4) Mentioned by Fantin-Latour.

Viscount Lepic in Place de la Concorde.
(1875) Zurich. Buhrle collection.
Handled like a Japanese print,
a page of Parisian comedy.

Theater Extras. (1877)
Paris, Louvre.
An habitué of theater wings and those of
the Opéra, Degas "voyeur" also
haunted the wings of the human soul.

THE COMMUNE, SOLITUDE AND AMERICA

It was with "un coeur léger," according to the then-President of the French Government Emile Ollivier, that France declared war on Prussia. But things soon took a different turn. The French army was ill-equipped and led by court favorites whose expertise was limited to incompetence and dishonesty. Faced with such a highly trained army, the French lost ground and Sedan quickly fell. Napoleon III recapitulated and the Third Republic began to organize the defense of the capital.

Manet and Degas, who had remained in Paris, joined the artillery division of the Garde Nationale. Manet became an officer under Meissonnier and though Degas was no supporter of the Republic, he joined the infantry. Owing to trouble with one of his eyes, he quickly passed into the artillery where he met up with an old acquaintance, Henri Rouart, who became an intimate friend.

Degas was a poor soldier, but willing enough. Later he confessed that he never even heard a cannon fire during his stint with the artillery division and was curious to know whether he would be able to bear the sound of his own equipment firing. Despite the many privations, the dangers and the vicissitudes of war, Manet and Degas made it to the house of Berthe Morisot, who made fun of her "warriors", saying that her future brother-in-law had "spent more time changing into his uniform" than actually fighting. As for Degas, she declared him "a bit crazy, but charming."

On September 19 the capital was suddenly under siege. Three weeks later, the French republican leader Léon Gambetta left a benumbed Paris to marshal defense forces in the provinces. The government withdrew and met at Bordeaux. Meanwhile, Paris was crippled by a lack of supplies and epidemic.

In his letters, Manet relates how they ate dogs, cats and rats. The more fortunate citizens ate horse meat. When winter set in the cold meted out many deaths among the desperate civilian population.

On January 5, 1871 the Prussians bombarded the

La Bouderie (Sulking). (1873/1875)
New York, Metropolitan Museum.
An example of the painter's experiments in naturalism.

Melancholy. (1874)
Washington, D. C., The Phillips Collection.
The artist's original use of light and composition on the diagonal
accentuates the model's anguished expression.

Interior or *The Rape.* (1874)
Philadelphia, MacIlhenny Collection.
A strange episode. Lighting effects similar to Expressionist cinema.
Naturalism already close to Félix Vallotton's.

city without respite, bringing it to its knees on January 24. France had lost the war. On March 1, the Prussians occupied the capital for a token eighteen hours. But the population was incensed by certain measures taken by the government, and chased its members out to Versailles. Meanwhile in Paris the Commune was hurriedly formed. In this state of agitation a new insurrectionist government was installed and all manner of passions were unleashed: *Courbet was elected to represent the people and made president of a general meeting of artists, which dismissed the Academy of Rome. the Ecole des Beaux-Arts, the Beaux-Arts section of the Institut and all the various medals issued by the Salon. The statute of the jury was left unchanged, however*[1].

At the Beaux-Arts Courbet quickly organized the demolition of the Vendôme Column celebrating Napoleon Bonaparte's victories and as such considered a symbol of his tyranny. For a second time, the city was under siege, this time at the hands of the political party from Versailles who, after systematically bombarding the capital from May 1, successfully stormed it on May 21. The reprisals were appalling, everywhere there were bloody encounters and acts of revenge. Courbet was imprisoned for his revolutionary activities.

As can be imagined, Degas was hardly in condition to take up his brushes. At a musical soirée held by Manet in July 1871, Berthe Morisot noted Degas in a corner, "asleep and utterly aged".

However, the artist was pursuing his study of musicians. Meanwhile, his repertoire widened with the painting *Ballet of Robert the Devil* and in July 1872 he stole a look behind the scenes and ventured into the changing rooms.

The grim tone of the post-Commune years gave the embittered Degas renewed interest in family life. While his Impressionist friends struggled among themselves for recognition, trying to impose the new techniques, one by one they also discovered the joy of establishing a family, a life with wife and children (such as Monet and Pissarro, despite all their debts). Degas meanwhile suffered a deepening solitude. In 1872, his brother René, who had moved to Louisiana in 1865, came to Europe and left this rather curious sketch of Edgar: *I found Edgar at the station to meet me, a matured man with a few wisps of gray hair in his beard; fatter and more sedate. We dined together and then went to see Marguerite. Edgar is doing some delightful things. He has made a portrait of Madame Camus in profile, wearing a red dress, sitting on a dark divan with a pink background: I think it a masterpiece. The style is captivating. Regrettably, his eyesight is failing and he has to be most careful. His cook is capable and he lives in a fine bachelor flat.*

Upon seeing René, Edgar succumbed to the desire to travel to New Orleans. Completely defying his stay-at-home nature, he felt that perhaps he could change a little and find new subjects for his painting. *Edgar has got it into his head to come back with me and stay for two months. He is planning all kinds of things regarding the natives and keeps asking questions about everyone. I think I shall take him with me. His eyes are better, but he will have to be careful. Now he is painting small canvases that tire his sight. He is currently painting a charming picture of a dance lesson.*

I must have it photographed in large format. I dine every day with him. His cook, Clotilde, is very capable. She dreams of coming to America. But she is too bright not to leave this job soon and find a well-to-do husband and install herself as a hostess somewhere. I would certainly bring her if it weren't for this possibility. After lunch I go with Edgar to the Champs Elysées and then on to a café-concert to listen to some idiotic songs, like the one about the Freemasons and other such rubbish.

When Edgar feels up to it, we go out into the country and visit the sites of the siege.

Prepare yourself to receive the great artists, so that Bruno and company, with the various dignitaries and clergy, do not turn up at the station to meet him[2].

One of Edgar's letters written during the Atlantic crossing relates his first impressions: *The ocean. How vast it is, and how far I am. The ship we are traveling in is a British vessel, swift and safe. In ten-twenty days it took us from Liverpool to the imperial city, New York. The crossing was depressing. I spoke no English and still don't and even when at sea the English continue with their aloofness and disregard for convention, perhaps you have experienced it. After four days' travel by rail, we finally reached our destination. I was fatter than upon my departure. There is nothing here but air, just air*[3].

In March 1873, Degas, relieved, crossed the threshold of his house once more. Clotilde had by now taken full command of the household and took advantage "of the first guest to arrive, asking him to step up on a stool and light the living-room gaslight".

Degas resumed work with renewed vigor: *"I only want to see this little corner of the world and make the very best of it. To achieve good results, one must stand at the balcony and stay there forever so as to watch everything that passes, everything around us, to experience it all agape*[4].

Ever faithful to his portraits, Degas wanted to recreate the environment around him. He composed complex scenarios in which the portrait was a mere pretext, such as *La Pédicure*, *La Bouderie*, *Melancholy*, and *Interior*. Then he passed on to outside settings, with *Portrait of Vicomte Lepic in Place de la Concorde*.

(1) John Rewald
(2) Letter home from René.
(3) Letter to Fröliche, November 27, 1872.
(4) Letter to Fröliche.

THE IMPRESSIONIST EPOPEE

It was Claude Monet who, in 1873, took up the idea first launched by Bazille in 1867, namely, to organize a group exhibition paid for by the artists themselves. Paul Alexis was of like mind: *As with every other association, the corporation of artists would be involved in organizing an artists' union and in setting up independent exhibitions.*

Other artists rallied to Monet's side: Camille Pissarro, Johan Barthold Jongkind, Alfred Sisley and Armand Guillaumin. In a note to the press, Alexis declared: *Most of these artists belong to the naturalist group, as they wish to paint nature and life as they are. But their association will not be a closed one. They want to unite their interests not their methods and trust that all those working in the sector will join them.*

Monet's scheme was well received, but just as it was about to be set up, objections were raised. The idea of an association of friends such as Corot, Daubigny and Courbet (in exile in Switzerland) was soon abandoned, and admitting anyone to the group, as suggested in Alexis' text, was out of the question.

Degas had reservations, given that the public would inevitably see such works as *refusés* or rejects. He advised those who exhibited at the Salon not to give such a revolutionary slant to the new initiative, so as to keep a lower profile and not lose the public's faith.

It was Pissarro who put forward the idea of a group association and chose to imitate the "charter" of the bakers' association as a model. Auguste Renoir was against having overly complex regulations and managed to have his way. Thus a simple common fund was set up in which each member paid a given quota to pay for overheads and expenses: *Pissarro also proposed a system that would guarantee each participant equal opportunity of having their works exhibited in the best position, so as to avoid discussions during the hanging. Lots were drawn for each picture, or votes were cast.*

In order to guarantee as even an arrangement as

Absinthe. (1876)
Paris, Louvre.
Less an anecdote than a flash of extraordinary violence.

Absinthe (detail).

possible, pictures were classified according to their dimensions, and then chance decided their actual position[1].

The first exhibition was held in rooms loaned by the photographer Nadar, situated at the corner of Rue Daunou and the Boulevard des Capucines. All the rooms had dark red plaster walls, and a grand staircase led straight from the Boulevard to the gallery.

Keen to attenuate the polemical tenor of the exhibition, Degas proposed to call it "Les Capucines". The title eventually chosen was "Société anonyme, coopérative, d'artistes, peintres, sculpteurs, graveurs" (Anonymous Cooperative Society of Artists, Painters, Sculptors and Engravers).

Monet, Renoir, Sisley, Pissarro and Berthe Morisot went canvasing for other adherents, though Degas himself was the most successful. He managed to convince Lepic, Levert, Rouart and de Nittis, whose participation was very important to Degas: "seeing as you all exhibit at the Salon, no one will be able to say that ours is just an exhibition of the *refusés*". Degas was particularly apprehensive about how the exhibition would be seen, and de Nittis was a kind of hostage.

He also tried to rope in Legros and Tissot, who were working in London. To the latter, Degas wrote: *Come come, my dear friend, do not hesitate, it will be to your advantage – this way you will show your works to Paris (which they believe you have shunned) and of course to us. Manet would like to set up something on his own, but I'm sure he would be sorry afterward. I saw the furnishings yesterday, the tones and the effect of daylight. It is as good as in other settings. Henner has shown up, he has just got through the second selection at the Salon but wants to exhibit with us. I am quite excited and keep track of everything, with a certain success, I believe. The newspapers have begun to print more than just small announcements, though there are no real articles as such just yet. The realist movement should not have adversaries. It exists and must find its place. There has to be a "Re-*

The Cotton Office. (1873)
Paris, Louvre.
This painting shows Degas' concern to depict an essential reality,
objective though still stereotyped.

alist Salon". Manet will not understand. I think he is more vain than intelligent.

For the first exhibition, a total of one hundred forty-five canvases were assembled. Renoir's brother Edmond was in charge of printing the catalogue. The titles put forward by Monet were somewhat uninspired: "Entrance to the Village," "Exit from the Village, "Morning in the Village." Edmond Renoir suggested some alternatives, at which Monet came up with the sudden idea of "impressions". No one could have imagined that this term would become so famous. The critics were hostile, and the word was repeated in derision. And so it was that, though not a school in itself, "Impressionism" became one of the most important artistic trends of the 19th century.

The vernissage took place on April 15, 1874 and stayed open far into the evening after normal viewing hours (an innovation for the times). Its success was largely due to a misunderstanding. The public went seeking amusement and the critics tried

to outdo each other in their attempts to pour ridicule on the exhibition.

The general hostility of the public and the press helped strengthen the bond between the exhibitors (though there were many points of disagreement among them) and gave the event a note of cohesion.

The artists had devised a means of defending themselves and guaranteeing exposure. Having been rejected by the official Salon, they had simply set up their own exhibition and financed it themselves.

The artists continued exhibiting side-by-side through until 1886, despite all their disagreements and the constant temptation to defect to the Salon and win prestige in the official art world.

The artists stuck together, spent their holidays together and made excursions to the same places, which is why we have their many versions of the same landscapes.

In Paris meanwhile they frequented the cafés, where there was a constant exchange and spread of

Women Outside a Café. (1877)
Paris, Louvre.
A vision presenting a group scene combined with atmosphere and amusing detail – a cinematographic painting.

ideas. They became café-goers out of necessity. The birth of the Impressionists and their movement is tied to the Café Guerbois, which for a full decade was the meeting point for all artists who were rejected by the official circles. When the Café Guerbois became too rowdy, the company moved to the Nouvelle Athènes in Place Pigalle, not far from the Cirque Fernando where Degas and Renoir habitually met. It was here in this café that Degas set his *Absinthe*, which he presented at the 1876 Impressionist Exhibition with the title of *In a Café*.

The raw realism of this painting had provoked a scandal when it was exhibited in London in 1873.

The ingenious arrangement of the tables creates a perspective that is interrupted by the undulating dress of the benumbed woman (the actress Ellen Andrée), while the man (Desboutin) is handled in a more energetic manner reminiscent of Courbet.

The Nouvelle Athènes was also the hideout of Desboutin, Manet, Forain, Henri Guérard (who was to marry Manet's pupil and friend Eva Gonzales in 1878), Duranty, Jean Richepin, Villiers de l'Isle Adam, Zola's disciple Alexis, Renoir and Pissarro. But the group had lost some of its steam since the heady days of the Café Guerbois. Manet and Sisley were rarely seen and Cézanne never. But the Nouvelle Athènes was the setting for the famous debate between Degas and Manet when their mutual friend de Nittis was awarded the Légion d'Honneur in 1878. Manet could not hide his disappointment at seeing yet another person receive the red band he had coveted for so long: *Degas would not brook certain forms of weakness – not out of modesty but because his overwhelming pride made him indifferent to external tokens of success and made him shrink from doing things which would make him stand out from the crowd.*

In his memoirs, de Nittis wrote that Manet *listened with a smile – almost a smirk – that made his nose curl. All this disdain, he told Degas, was insincere. "You have everything, and I am happy about that. In our hearts, we have all awarded each other a* *golden medal, together with other more flattering gifts. If there were no compensations, I would not invent them, but they exist. You have to have what distinguishes you from the masses when you can. I have no official decorations, but that's not my doing. I would have if I could and will do my utmost to get one".* At this point, Degas thundered *"Well, I already knew how bourgeois you were!"*

Georges Moore, an old pupil of Cabanel, a young Irishman whom Degas painted and who has left some pungent descriptions of Parisian life, tells of how Degas used to arrive at the café late, around ten in the evening. *For those who knew him, his stooping, slightly swaying gait, tweed clothes and baritone voice were all quite unique. His conversation was usually sprinkled with aphorisms and he was less interested in helping the new generation artists than his friends Pissarro and Renoir were.*

Indeed, his advice to artists just beginning was to work from memory alone.

The second Impressionist Exhibition at the Durand-Ruel galleries in April 1876 was not as successful as the first. It consisted of works by twenty artists, with two hundred fifty-three paintings, pastels, watercolors, drawings and etchings. The public continued to see the young artists as a band of clowns. Degas presented twenty-four works, including one he painted in New Orleans, the large *Cotton Office*, which was supposed to be exhibited at the Musée de Pau in 1878 and had nothing Impressionistic about it.

Albert Wolf recorded the public's reaction in the daily *Le Figaro: The Rue Le Peletier is certainly unlucky. After the blaze at the Opéra, now there's another disaster: the Durand-Ruel gallery has just opened what is supposed to be an exhibition of paintings. The unwitting passer-by, drawn in by the flags along the building's façade is suddenly faced by an astonishing, cruel spectacle: five or six ostracized people, including a woman, a motley group of ambition-crazed wretches who have teamed up to exhibit their work. Some people simply burst out laugh-*

ing when they see their work. I confess that it disturbs me. These so-called artists have dubbed themselves "intransigents" or "impressionists": they take the canvas and then daub the paint on at random, then sign it.

A truly horrible spectacle of human vanity run amok to the point of lunacy.

After attacking Pissarro, Wolf turned on Degas: *Try reasoning with Degas! Tell him that he has some fine qualities, drawing skills, a command of color and execution. He will simply laugh in your face and call you a reactionary.*

The compliments were gratuitous. Degas's brilliant classical execution was his hallmark. No one was as attentive to style as Degas. The critic was hardly objective in lumping all the artists together. The exhibition served as a pretext for an article by Duranty (*La Nouvelle Peinture: a propos du groups d'artistes qui expose dans les galleries Durand-Ruel*), in which he examined the problem of realism and expressed the ideas of Degas, who he claimed was the source of the theories he had developed. Ever since 1856, Duranty had tried to focus certain trends common to both literature and painting. Like the de Goncourts and Zola, he stressed the importance of closely observing the modern world: *I have witnessed the society, facts and deeds, the professors and other figures of various different spheres. I have seen comic moments, gestures and faces that ought to have been captured in paint. I have seen groups of people interacting among themselves when they meet in different moments of life – in church, in the dining room, in the drawing room, at the cemetery, on the parade ground, in the studio, in the Chambre, everywhere.*

The difference of behavior, the physical variety, the individual walk, feelings and actions are all essential components. Everything seemed organized as if the world were created solely to delight the eye, created for the sheer delight of painters.

Besides Degas, only Manet (and earlier Courbet) had shown an interest in removing the barriers between art and daily life.

But Degas was not an entirely objective witness of his times: *Degas felt that something he had observed could not be painted before it had been "rectified or critically assessed by his mind. For him, in the words of Alfred de Vigny, art is a reality chosen beforehand. The components [of his vision] were dictated beforehand, unconsciously determined by his disillusionment and resentments. He made his choices to satisfy a kind of wistful melancholy, tending toward misanthropy and misogyny, severity, reproach, sarcasm. Whether the subject was dancing girls or singers from the café, angry women, seemingly offended women à la toilette or absinthe drinkers, his art was neither objective nor impartial, it offered no proof, just judged and stigmatized*[2].

As he expanded his range of inquiry, Degas explored new settings and situations: the music hall, the café-concerts, even the circus. "You may prefer natural life", he explained to his colleagues, "but I prefer an artificial one"[3]. This comment alone is enough to distinguish him from the Impressionists. "I have always tried to urge my colleagues to look for new combinations in style rather than in color itself", he continued. "But they have preferred not to pay any attention and pursue other goals"[4].

Degas felt that his Impressionist friends were too tied to nature. He did not approve of their utter fidelity to the subject they were painting, nor of their basic principle of leaving nothing out, changing nothing, nor of their eagerness to fix the immediate sensations. *It is fine to copy what you see, but better to depict what you can only see in your mind's eye. In this moment of transformation, the imagination colludes with memory. You only reproduce the things that most struck you, that is, the essentials. Your memories and your imagination are thus freed from the tyranny of nature*[5].

Paradoxically, while the Impressionist finished his canvas in one sitting, while the emotion was still fresh, Degas worked in his studio with an obsession for perfection. He was never satisfied with his work, and hesitated before selling a canvas or begged his clients to return certain paintings to him for further touching up. On one occasion, this excess of scrupulousness over his work had unpleasant consequences. A singer called Faure (whose portrait Manet had painted) had purchased six canvases from the Durand-Ruel galleries. But Degas was not entirely satisfied with these works and proposed to swap the six paintings for four other compositions. Two of these were delivered in 1876, but after insisting and eventually threatening Degas, the singer was obliged to take him to court for the other two.

Women outside a Cafè in the Evening dates from the same period as *Absinthe*, but marks a turning point in Degas's art. He gave up his smooth and contained handling of his paints, though not his firm and vigorous forms, and began to experiment with a more open feel, with bold dashes of pastel, clustered to give the subject a kind of rough immediacy that was later to become his hallmark.

Undoubtedly, Degas was influenced by his colleagues and by their more free and rapid execution, by their nervous and impulsive expression which until then had been so different from his own.

Now, the former accuracy of form was replaced by an intense investigation into pain. His preoccupation with realism and his prejudices on composition (which were linked to his parallel research into photography) began to show. *What can we say about this Parisian thoroughbred whose works express such keen literary and philosophical talent on top of his skill with color and form? A single stroke says more about him than any words can–his work is spiritual, refined and genuine. Degas is by no means naive, as some may suppose. His considerable knowledge is manifest everywhere. He ingeniously slots his figures in the most unpredictable and amusing manner, yet their positions always seem real and normal. What Degas really dislikes is romantic blandness, the replacement of life with dreams or, put more dramatically, the spectacle. He is the kind of observer who avoids exaggeration. The effect he wants is achieved on its own, without being forced.*

This is why he has become such a prized "historian" of the scenes he depicts: witness his women at the cafè doorways in the evening, or the sheer poetry of the woman tapping her fingernail against her teeth and saying "pas seulement ça." Another woman rests a gloved hand on a small table. Behind her the crowded Boulevard tapers away into the distance[6].

With great simplicity, Rivière captures a glimpse of the novelty of Degas's vision, the utter originality and modernism of his pictorial expression. The descriptions of the works are not an anticipation of the intentions of the artist, as may have seemed earlier. The words Rivière imagines the woman in the picture saying are the only thing one can imagine her saying, while her friend in the gloves adds an intense note of truth to the scene, a moment of keen observation and psychological insight. Neither must we overlook Rivière's mention of the receding noise of the Boulevard. The picture is like a frame from a film, an instant fixed in time and space with all its sensory context.

The scenographer has omitted nothing, the careful choice of elements captures the moment in all its *fragile densitè*.

Instead of presenting us with a series of photographic "frames," Degas has highlighted all the more explicit details in a single exposure, to create an almost hallucinatory scene.

In the evenings, he would make forays into the Paris night-life, observing the effect of the cruel artificial light on the passers-by (such as in *The Cafè-Concert des Ambassadeurs*), fixing the same subjects Manet had done earlier. But his very individual perception of the world of dance heralded a completely new genre, a new vision.

Degas ably captured and savored that succulent mixture of real and fictitious, that strange amalgam of prosaic and poetic, all the possibilities this theme offered, a theme that even inspired him to write a verse:

En vous la danse a mis quelque chose d'à part
Hèroique et lointain. On sait de votre place
Que les reines se fondent de distance et de fard[7].

This kind of annotation was typical of Degas, who considered women as something quite inaccessible, even artificial.

The third Impressionist Exhibition was held in an empty apartment on the second floor of Rue Le Peletier (in the same street as the Durand-Ruel galleries) and a total of eighteen painters participated with two hundred thirty works. Degas sent twenty-five paintings, pastels and lithographs depicting dancers, café-concert scenes and women *à la toilette*. He was given a room of his own at the back of the suite. The exhibition was slated by the critics, but new adherents came forward and their numbers grew. That same year, the new recruits included Paul Gauguin and Mary Cassatt. Cassatt was particularly fond of Degas' work, who had first noticed her contribution at the Salon in 1874. Mary Cassatt was the daughter of a Pittsburgh banker and in 1868 she had traveled through Europe before settling in Paris to devote herself to her painting, renouncing her material welfare.

She met Degas, who invited her to exhibit with the Impressionists. She was overjoyed to be able to finally work independently, without having to worry about the opinion of a jury.

Though she was never actually a pupil of Degas, she was influenced by his work. *They had the same intellectual mentality, the same predilection for form, but she added a mixture of sentiment and cool vivacity that were part of her nature*[8].

Mary Cassatt was represented in the fourth Impressionist Exhibition in 1879, held in No.28, avenue de l'Opéra.

This time, in compliance with Degas' wishes, the group omitted the word "impressionist" on the posters advertising the event. The group accepted a text suggested by Degas, which simply announced the fourth exhibition of a group of independent artists.

Writing in *Vie Moderne*, critic Armand Silvestre ridiculed the venture, saying: *The public is invited to witness the funeral service and burial of the Im-*

pressionists. This sad invitation comes from the new Independents. No false tears, no false rejoicing. Just calm. There is no mention of death. These artists have decided that the word they originally chose for themselves meant nothing, and so have chosen another.

Besides Mary Cassatt and Federigo Zandomeneghi, Degas also managed to involve Jean Louis Forain and had even proposed including Raffaelli, though this suggestion was strongly rejected by all.

The number of artists adhering to the Impressionists continued to rise. The brief success of Renoir at the Salon (he had shunned the Impressionist Exhibition) prompted Monet to try his hand once more for official recognition. Degas remained utterly indifferent to Monet's arguments (which were strictly practical, being without the material means Degas had at his disposal) and saw it as a breach of faith, declaring this concession to officialdom an odious defection. Degas accused his colleague of "publicity-seeking" and abruptly severed relations with him.

In the meantime, Renoir, Sisley, Cézanne and Monet dropped out of the fifth Exhibition organized in 1880, which could no longer call itself "Impressionist". Degas failed to garner the adhesion of Raffaelli, Levert, Rouart, Tissot and Vidal, his friends.

The exhibition was held at No. 10, Rue des Pyramides in April. On Degas' suggestion, the event was presented as an exhibition of independent artists. But his advice was not followed for the exhibition posters, as he complained to Bracquemond: *We open on April 1. The posters are going up tomorrow or Monday. They are in red letters on a green background. There was a row with Caillebotte whether to put our names on or not. When will the bickering cease? Mlle Cassatt and Mme Morisot did not want to figure on the poster. Neither sound reasoning nor simple good taste seem to have any effect on the general laziness nor on Caillebotte's stub-*

bornness. *Next year I shall make sure none of this happens, it is depressing, humiliating.*

Among the works Degas put on display (which do not correspond with those in the catalogue) was a portrait of Duranty, who had died shortly before. This time, the public was no longer hostile, just indifferent. The exhibition attracted few visitors and there was little derision. A split began to form within the group, with the friends of Pissarro (the only one to remain faithful to Berthe Morisot), Guillaumin and Gauguin on one side, and Degas' clique on the other with Forain, Raffaelli and Zandomeneghi, whose work (like that of Degas himself) no longer had anything impressionist about it at all.

When moves were made in 1881 to set up a sixth Impressionist Exhibition, the gap between Caillebotte and Degas widened.

Caillebotte felt that the introduction of Degas' artist friends was giving the group an increasingly Classical slant.

Furthermore, he thought that Degas was too harsh in his judgments of Monet and Renoir. In a letter to Pissarro, he wrote: *What are our exhibitions to become? Quite frankly, I feel we must keep to a specific artistic direction, working single-mindedly in the direction that serves everyone's interests. I therefore ask that the exhibition be made up of the works of those who have truly worked toward this end, namely, yourself, Monet, Renoir, Sisley, Morisot, Cassatt, Cézanne, Guillaumin, Gauguin if you like, myself and perhaps Cordey. That is all, but Degas rejects such an exhibition outright. I don't think the public is very interested in our internal wrangling. It is quite absurd to fight like this. Degas has upset our organization. It is a pity that he has such a bad character. He spends all his time at the Nouvelle Athènes or in high society. He ought to paint more. Of course he is right when he says that he speaks with a deep understanding of painting. This is the basis of his reputation. But we mustn't forget that the real argument of any painter is his work itself, and while he may reason well, it would be more appropriate to get down to work. He now invokes certain existential needs that he won't however extend Renoir and Monet. But before he lost money was he so different from what he is today? We should ask all those who know him. He is very bitter that he does not really have the status that his vast talent deserves. He would never admit it, of course, but he seems to be angry with the world. He claims that he only wanted Raffaelli and the others after Renoir and Money defected.*

And yet he plagued Raffaelli for three years to join us, long before Renoir and Monet actually went. He insists we keep together and count on each other, yet look who he wants to join: Lepic, Legros and Maureau...

He did not protest when Lepic and Legros defected. Lepic had no talent anyway. In the meantime, he will not forgive Renoir, Sisley and Monet because they are talented. In 1878 he brought Zandomeneghi to the group, then Bracquemond and his wife, and then Raffaelli in 1879. This bunch is simply fighting for realism. If anyone has the right not to forgive Sisley, Renoir, Monet and Cézanne it is your group, because you have the same material problems as they have, but have not given in. You are more straightforward, more correct than Degas. And the reason is simply a question of survival. When we need money, we find a way round. Degas is happy to argue over basic issues that I find above discussion. He seems to have a persecution mania. Maybe he wants to imply that Renoir's ideas are Machiavellian. This is unfair and very ungenerous. I have no right to accuse anyone in this affair, only you have the right to do that. I will say, however, that this upright citizen Degas has railed all his life against everyone and anyone with talent. You could fill a book with what he has said about you, Manet and Monet. Shouldn't we be helping each other, excusing our various weaknesses rather than destroying each other? In the meantime, the one person who has talked so much and made great plans is the very one who has personally contributed the least. It is all very saddening. If discussions

Women Combing Their Hair.
Washington, D. C., The Phillips Gallery.

between us had concentrated solely on art, we would certainly have all got along together. It was Degas who began to bring up other issues, and it would be folly to give into this madness. True enough, he has enormous talent. But that is all. Just think he has even had the gall to ask me if I allow Renoir and Monet to set foot in my house! For all his talent, he has an appalling character.

In conclusion, if you want to set up a purely artistic exhibition, I have no idea of how we'll go about it next year. We'll have to see what happens in the coming two months. If Degas wants to take part, so be it. But without all the other people that trail behind him. The only friends of his that could qualify are Rouart and Tissot⁹.

Despite these criticisms, Pissarro took sides with Degas and Caillebotte withdrew.

The sixth Impressionist Exhibition signaled the victory of Degas' group. It opened in April 1881 at No. 35, Boulevard des Capucines in a section of the building in which the photographer Nadar had installed his studio. Degas presented fewer paintings this time, but included a small piece of sculpture entitled *Little Ballerina of Fourteen.*

In 1881 the undaunted Caillebotte began to encourage his friends to put on a new exhibition featuring members of the original group. He met with Rouart, one of Degas' close friends, who agreed to try and dissuade Degas from inviting Raffaelli et al. In fact, Raffaelli's work had no place among the Impressionists.

Despite his efforts, Caillebotte failed. He wrote to Pissarro, not without a hint of resentment, saying that Degas would not give up Raffaelli, especially if asked.

On December 14, Pissarro also heard from Paul Gauguin: *Degas has informed me that he would rather withdraw than reneg on Raffaelli. Looking objectively at the situation after ten years of working together on these exhibitions, I notice that the number of Impressionists has increased, that they represent the more talented and more influential part of the group. As for Degas, the trend he has created is a bad sign: each year an Impressionist leaves his place for a completely vacuous newcomer, students from the École. In two years' time he will find himself surrounded by confidence tricksters of the first order. Your efforts are quite in vain and Durand-Ruel has lost the market. In spite of my good nature, I can no longer continue to put up with Raffaelli and company. Would you please, therefore, accept my resignation. From today, I will take a back seat.*

After Gauguin's resignation, Pissarro found himself in a very tight spot. An exhibition without the contribution of Cézanne, Sisley, Renoir, Monet, Caillebotte, Gauguin and Guillaumin would no longer impress and had little meaning. There remained only Berthe Morisot to represent the original, authentic impressionist vocation. Pissarro had to make a choice between his life-long friends, and the bullying Degas and his following.

Gauguin offered further insights into the situation: *You keep saying that I am impatient and want things quick, but you must admit that in this affair my forecasts were right. No one can dissuade me that for Degas, Raffaelli is simply a pretext for provoking a split. Degas has the habit of seeing ill-will where it simply does not exist. He seems bent on destroying everything. Reflect on this, will you, and act accordingly.*

Attempts to persuade Monet, Renoir, Morisot and Cassatt (who was asked to exhibit without Degas) were unsuccessful and Caillebotte was just about to give up when Durand-Ruel, the Impressionists' official dealer, stepped in to handle the organization of the exhibition, which he felt in keeping with his personal policy.

Various letters were exchanged and the group almost reformed. Degas dropped out because his protégés were not included. Rouart, who had paid the rental of the room himself withdrew also, and with him Mary Cassatt, in solidarity. The exhibition eventually opened on March 1, 1882, in No. 251, Rue Saint Honoré.

Manet was present at the vernissage and wrote to his wife: *I found a crowd of Impressionists busy hanging pictures in a huge hall. Degas has remained part of the association, pays his quota but has entered none of his works. The association continues to bear the name "Independents" which he himself gave it.*

After eight years of wrangling and discussions, this seventh exhibition of the series was the most coherent and the members managed to put together a fully representative exhibition of Impressionist art. A few months before his death, at the close of the 1882 Salon, Edouard Manet finally received the decoration he had so eagerly awaited, the Légion d'Honneur.

During the winter, his failing health prevented him from embarking on any large-scale project and he made do with some pastel sketches. Finally, he was forced to retire to bed and his strength left him. He was assisted by Dr. Gachet, a good friend to many painters, whose home in d'Auvers-sur-Oise had become a retreat for many artists, Cézanne and Van Gogh in particular. Gachet was against amputating Manet's leg, which was too late and Manet died on April 30. Degas was shattered by Manet's death and declared his friend "was greater than we imagined." This loss and the withdrawal of the main members of the group to the provinces meant that in Paris itself there was no effective Impressionists group to speak of. Renoir and Monet, meanwhile, roamed the south of the country in search of new stimuli. Cézanne retired to Aix. Pissarro and Sisley stayed out in the countryside of the Ile de France with barely enough money to make the occasional trip into Paris. They no longer felt the need to gather in the cafés. In a last bid to gather the group again, Duret, Mallarmé and Huysmans decided to organize an "Impressionist dinner" at least once a month in Paris. Attendance at these get-togethers varied greatly. Some artists abstained. Degas, the only Parisian (and the wealthiest), turned up regularly but was more morose than ever. Biographer John Rewald explains that as Degas grew older, his cantankerousness became increasingly evident. He

loved this contact with the others, the exchange of ideas, but at fifty he felt himself to be an old man and wanted to live like one, embittered and awfully nauseated by life. A letter to a friend confirms this impression. Speaking of himself, he wrote: *You close shut, like a door, and not just with your friends. You suppress everything around you and, once alone, you kill yourself out of sheer disgust.*

I have made many projects, but here I am, immobile and impotent. I seem to have lost the thread of things. I always thought I had time for everything. I always imagined I would get round to doing the things I put off or was as hampered by my eye trouble and all the other problems I had. I kept stockpiling my plans in a cupboard and carried the key with me. It now looks as if I have mislaid the key. I fear that I will never be able to shrug off this comatose state I have fallen into. Like so many others. I keep saying "I will see to it," and then do nothing[10].

In 1886 Berthe Morisot and her husband Eugène Manet began mobilizing for a new exhibition of Im-

pressionist art. As usual, they encountered hurdles with Degas and then Pissarro, who wanted to invite two newcomers, Georges Seurat and Paul Signac.

Degas was keen to organize the exhibition for May 15, the inauguration day of the official Salon. Manet and Morisot declined to participate and were replaced by Guillaumin. Pissarro realized that without Degas, Cassatt and Morisot, the only people able to actually finance the installations, there was not much that could be done. When Raffaelli, who was the main cause of the rifts in the first place, realized that the Impressionists were not keen on his participation, he withdrew of his own accord: *Degas decided to give up Raffaelli without a fuss at all, because no one had in fact asked him to do so.*

The problem now was Seurat and Signac. Pissarro wrote to his son Lucien: *I don't give a jot about what or which artist is good, and cannot accept the airy-fairy judgments of these romantics who are keen to crush the new currents. I accept the challenge, but even before we have begun they are busy shuffling the cards and ruin-*

Mane of Hair
Paris, Louvre, Drawing Exhibition Room.

Woman at Her Bath, Sponging Her Leg. (1893)
Paris, Louvre.
An exquisite, supple and sensual line.

Woman Combing Her Hair. (1885)
Paris, private collection.
A thematic of gestuality forms around the woman's figure which
functions more as its axis than its core.

The Tub.
Paris, Louvre.
A streak of "voyeurism."

Young Woman in a Café.
New York, Stralem Collection.
The pathos of solitude.

ing the exhibition's chances. Manet was beside himself. I certainly won't get over it. What a lot of underhand dealings. But I'll hang on. Degas is a hundred times more faithful. I told Degas that Seurat's painting is most interesting, and I should know! What mastery! And if Degas can see nothing in it, then that's his loss. There's something unusual in it that escapes him[11].

When Gauguin returned from Denmark, where he had blended into the community and painted scenes from social and family life, he was ready to exhibit.

However, he had previously met Degas in Normandy and they had fallen out.

The incompatibility of the two artists was great: Degas scorned what he felt was Gauguin's opportunism and social climbing. In turn, the latter considered Degas hopelessly bourgeois.

Later on, in a letter to Schuffenecker, he would declare: *As for Degas, I am not interested in nor intend spending my life honing down my art according to his model. The price is too high.*

With some difficulty, after the withdrawal of Monet, Caillebotte, Renoir and Sisley, the exhibition was prepared. Degas wrote to Bracquemond: *It is due to open on the fifteenth. Everything is being done in a mad hurry. The only condition for admittance is that artists are not exhibiting at the Salon. You do not qualify, but what about your wife? Monet, Renoir, Caillebotte and Sisley have not rallied to the call. The expenses are being covered by a system too complicated to explain here. If the takings don't cover the expenses, we will pass a hat round among those exhibiting. The rooms are small but well lit. It is the first floor of the Maison Dorée on the corner of Rue Laffitte. The Jablochkof company has suggested we use electric lighting.*

In this eighth Impressionist Exhibition, which was the last, Degas exhibited a series of seven pastels: *Suite de Nus de femmes se baignant, se lavant, se séchant, s'essuyant, se peignant ou se faisant peigner.* Together with Seurat's *The Grande Jatte,* these pastels manage to cause an uproar.

Woman Drying Herself. (1903)
New York, Paul Rosenberg Collection.
Three moments of the same gesture. This work reminds us of
Muybridge's photographic experiments in which he studied the
successive stages of a movement.

Woman Seated on the Edge of a Tub.
Paris, private collection.

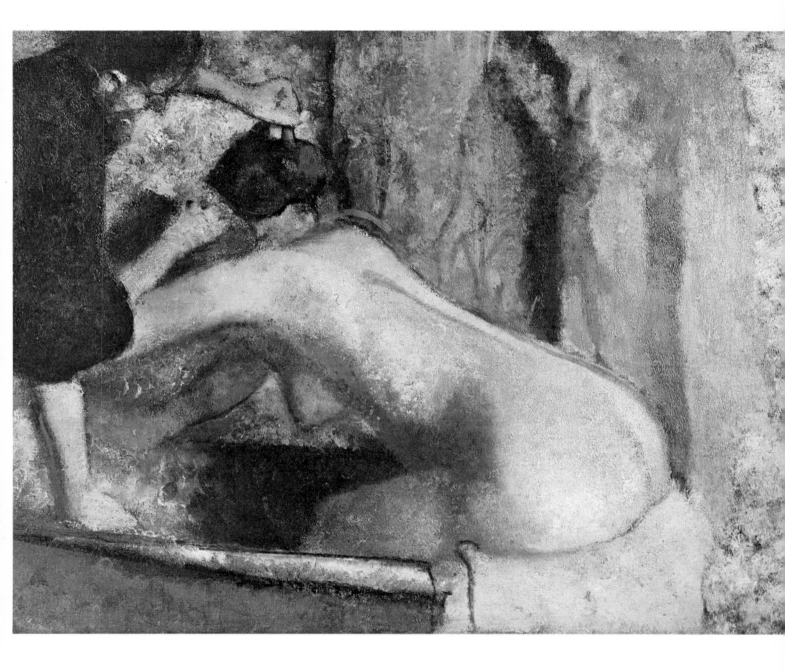

When Emile Verhaeren expressed his enthusiasm, his colleagues thought he was bluffing.

Meanwhile, thanks to the determined efforts of Durand-Ruel and Mary Cassatt, Impressionism found a receptive audience in the United States. The critics were divided over Degas. Some declared his hand "mediocre," others greatly admired him for "his deep knowledge of art and for his superior acquaintance with life itself".

(1) John Rewald. *Histoire de l'Impressionnisme.*
(2) Jean Louis Vaudoyer. *Les Impressionnistes.*
(3) Quoted by Georges Moore.
(4) Quoted by Walter Sickert. "Degas." *Burlington Magazine*, November 1917.
(5) G. Jeanniot. "Souvenirs de Degas." *La Revue Universale* 1933.
(6) First issue of the magazine *Impressionniste.*
(7) P.A. Lemoisne.
(8) John Rewald.
(9) Quoted in John Rewald. *Histoire de l'Impressionnisme.*
(10) Quoted in John Rewald.
(11) John Rewald.

A BOURGEOIS GENTILHOMME (II)

When his father died in 1874, Degas' financial situation looked to be in a shambles. Achille and his uncle Musson rushed over from New Orleans to salvage the family's honor.

In the first place, Renè was obliged to return the sum of money loaned him to open the De Gas Brothers company. Degas came to his aid and, as a means of paying back his brother's debts, he resigned himself to toning down his lifestyle and selling a few pieces from his prized art collection.

Although he was generally considered to be selfish, Degas proved to be most considerate, generous and understanding. But there were more troubles on the horizon. René left his wife to marry a certain Mrs. Leonce Olivier, née America Durrive. Where Degas had shown such thoughtfulness for his brother's financial plight, in this instance he broke off all relations with him.

The new element in the life of Degas, according to Louis Vauxcelles, was that he was suddenly forced to think of his works as salable assets, as a kind of currency for meeting his most elementary needs. Degas' economic position became ambiguous. As a bourgeois gentleman he was highly reserved, even in moments of dire difficulty. As he was considered rich, he had to struggle to live decorously, while his colleagues Pissarro, Monet and Sisley, being of a lower social standing and decidedly "Bohemian", had no difficulty making public their hardships and openly asked others for help.

What was Degas like during this period of melancholy and financial straits? The accounts left by his colleagues are contradictory in places. Hence, the man who was described by Paul Lafond as being somewhat short, is depicted by Georges Rivière as *a tallish man, above average height, well-proportioned, distinguished-looking. He held his head high naturally and joined his hands behind his back whenever he stood conversing. Degas dressed finely, without any trace of eccentricity; like all bourgeois men of the era, he wore a tall hat with a wide brim, perched slightly on the back of his head. He usually screened his eyes behind a pair of dark glasses which straddled a rather short nose. His face was framed by long chestnut-colored sideburns which he kept clipped, along with the rest of his beard and hair.*

Degas lived near Place Pigalle, but during the period of the Impressionist Exhibitions he moved to No. 4, Rue Frochot: *a small villa with a front garden, with a sturdy acacia which in spring cast a dense shadow over the house. The artist lived alone with an old maidservant and a growling guard-dog. This bachelor's apartment was somewhat drab and the furniture bourgeois, sober and a little Jansenist, as was the fashion then. Degas never thought of adding any imaginative touches to the house, though at the time painters and romantic writers competed among each other for medieval junk of all kinds. He was in no way drawn to eccentric interiors or décor. Despite his liberal views on art, he was bourgeois through-and-through, fussy about order both inside and out-side the house, a true conservative who loved good manners and the simplicity of the family setting. His motto might well have been nothing obtrusive.*

A solitary soul, hard-working, shunning the night life and ever faithful to his friends. Daniel Halévy, son of Degas' close friend Ludovic, wrote: *He was an unfailing friend. To attend a funeral or embrace someone, Degas was prepared to brave a fifteen hour train journey. Yet all this was hidden behind a stiff and apparently insensitive exterior, a queer but wholly superficial coarseness.*

With his grating ways and biting phrases, Degas screened himself from intruders. He wanted to de-vote himself entirely to his research. *If I did not be-have so, people would never leave me a moment to work. I am shy by nature and have to force myself to be tough.*

With some regret, he noted: *Those who are content to observe themselves can hardly be happy.*

But there was also bitterness: *I am completely bogged down in my studies. I see too little of the people I love and sooner or later this will begin to weigh on me.*

Ever since the days of the Cafè Guerbois, Degas had unfailingly attended the café sessions. Later, after the death of Manet in 1883, the Nouvelle Athènes began to fill with writers and painters and Degas continued to make his presence felt. There he was to meet Auguste Renoir, Desboutin, Forain, Zandomeneghi, Jeanniot, Lafond, Gervex, Humbert, Gèrome and Cormon.

Degas was very fond of toying with ideas. Many biographers have noted his caustic wit, noting his rather blunt and forward remarks about people he did not like. Indeed, he had one of the most feared tongues of Paris. He was the kind of person one in-vited to one's table just to hear him cast aspersions on the various public figures of the moment and dis-parage the ideas of certain artists. But they were the protests of an adamantly bourgeois mind, intolerant toward the Jews, toward the "Bohemians" and any-one else who failed to observe the law or live with a sense of dignity and honor. Some of his remarks be-came legendary. Degas is said to have called Renoir "a cat playing with a ball of wool".

Besnard, he said, was "a fireman who has caught fire himself" and Meissonnier a "giant among dwarves." He made malicious comments about Emile Zola. When a friend told Degas he was worried about having to transport certain paintings of an art-ist Degas did not like, he was told not to worry, "they're deflatable." He used turns of phrase that are often quoted to typify his irritable character. Valéry recalls having found Degas at Henri Rouart's house: *Each Friday, Degas would faithfully present himself, full of steam and habitually insufferable, to animate Rouart's dinners. He would lash out with his wit, in-stilling amusement and terror. He would pass judg-ment, mimic people, make biting quips, invent apologues, make the most astonishing series of lucid, passionate and self-confident wise-cracks. He in-variably slated the literary elite, the Institut, the fake hermits and latest arrived among the artists: he quoted freely from Saint-Simon, Proudhon, Racine and from the odd sayings of Ingres. I believe I understand him.*

His "Amphitryon" looked on in loving admiration. *The other dinner guests–young people, old generals, silent society ladies– registered mixed reactions at the* tour de force *of irony and aesthetics, at the indefatigable wit of this wordmonger.*

As it happened, Degas was very keen on literature and, though he failed to grasp Mallarmé, was friends with a number of poets. He even wrote a set of sonnets, which are as precise as his drawings, but somewhat dry. In a letter to Berthe Morisot, Mallarmé declared: *At the moment he is rather distracted by his poetry–this winter he was busy on his fourth sonnet. He has stopped going out and it is fascinating to see him tackling this new art medium, which he does with splendid results[1].*

Degas clearly had a literary bent. His letters to Rouart, Bartholomé, Ludovic Halévy and Durand-Ruel, to Suzanne Valadon, all written to arrange or cancel some rendezvous, are full of humor and quick, precise observations. At times, his sarcasm was a cover for his own embarrassment. He adored engineering his phrases and was a great lover of games: we know from photographs that he had plans for various one-act plays he wanted to produce. At the house of his friends Valpinçon in the summer of 1894, he attended a performance of a play he had no role in. He wrote to Bartholomé: *To hide my disappointment and make myself useful I composed a small piece in blank verse. Nobody understood it because it was too refined, but they did pick up its gallant undertone, which has always been my prerogative.*

In his preface to his uncle's eight sonnets, Jean Nepveu-Degas explained: *When he read the texts of "Tiroir de Laque" (a collection Mallarmé wanted to publish with illustrations by Renoir, Monet, Berthe Morisot and Degas), this precise and difficult art, which was absolutely new to him, awakened a desire. Drawn by the difficulties he foresaw and keen to demonstrate to himself what was behind a work of art, he insisted that it was a question of will-power: if one wanted, one could be a poet.*

Berthe Morisot was not impressed by Degas' verses, and wondered "Sont-ils poétiques? ou des variantes sur le tub?" However, they do illustrate many of the artist's enduring and deep-felt preoccupations: *In fact the poems tie in with some of Degas' favorite topics: horses, ballerinas, women washing, like a verbal transposition of his painting, embellished by his implacable visual insights[2].*

It is symptomatic that Degas chose the sonnet as his means of setting will against whim and to illustrate the difference between intention and impressions regarding a finished work, forcing the onlooker to see content and form as one and the same thing. In his poetry as in his painting, Degas invariably sought out difficulty: *He only valued whatever involved a great effort. It was the work itself that excited him. For Degas, the work of the poet as he kept striving for the version of the text that met specific requirements seemed to be similar to that of the artist drawing what he conceived.*

(1) Ouoted by Henri Mondor in *Vie de Mallarmé.*
(2) Pierre Cabanne.

Degas on the street.
(photo courtesy Bibliothèque Nationale)

THE PARIS STALKER

More than any other city, with its daily human spectacle, promenades and picturesque corners, Paris never ceased to arrest Degas' attention. He occasionally went out to the country, but always returned to his favorite part of town, livlng variously in Rue Fontaine Saint Georges, Rue Pigalle, Rue Ballu (in a hotel where Zola had once lived), Rue Victor Massé and finally settling in Boulevard Clichy. Gustave Coquiot wrote that Degas *never left home unless he desperately needed rest and a change of air. He always came back grumpy, full of complaints, angry at having to get back to work, to his painstaking work that required repeating sketches many times over to achieve anything worthwhile. The worst of these trips was the one he took with Boldini to Tangiers. He came back nauseated, a total wreck. When he and his friend left each other at the Gare de Lyon, he determined never to see him again, and in fact he never did.*

Deep down, Degas disliked both Paris and himself. He often set out on long rides, taking his hypochondria with him like some dog on a leash; anyone who came across him without recognizing him would find himself in trouble. One of his favorite treats was to take a round trip on the platform of a tram or the top deck of the omnibus.

Nonetheless, Degas was constantly absorbed by Paris and knew every nook and cranny. Coquiot was curious to find out exactly where Degas went on his walks. The painter had a great many favorite routes, including the Batignolles to the Odéon, the Panthéon to Place de Courcelles, Notre Dame de Lorette to Jardin des Plantes, Montrouge to Gare de Passy, Porte d'Ivry to the Bastille, Rue de Sèvres to Gare du Nord, Porte de Vincennes to Porte de Saint-Cloud. *One of the routes he took most frequently ran from the Louvre to Lac de Saint Fargeau. Lurching along and loaded up as if bound for some distant land, the two-horse omnibus clattered up Rue du Louvre, Rue Saint Honoré, Rue Croix des Petits Champs, Place des Victoires, Rue d'Aboukir, Rue du Caire, Rue Saint Denis, the Porte*

Saint Denis and the Boulevard, Porte Saint Martin and the Boulevard, Place de la République, Faubourg du Temple, rue de la Fontaine au Roi, Avenue Parmentier, Rue Deguerry, Rue Saint Maur, Rue de l'Orillon, Boulevard de Belleville. Near breaking point, the tram would groan to a halt at Lac de Saint Fargeau. Here Degas would watch the people's faces, making mental notes of their expressions and gestures. He breathed in the Paris air, impregnating himself with sensations that he would later try and translate into images in his studio.

He did the same thing when he wanted to paint cafè-concert scenes. Once again, Coquiot provides us with a close description of Degas' interests and movements: Degas began to frequent the cafè-concerts assiduously from 1885 through to 1889. All his sketches of singers at the concert cafés date from this period. He followed the thundering Thérèsa and her songs "J'ai tué mon capitaine", "La femme à barbe", "La Marseillaise", and others. He makes note of all the various types of singer and their diction and delivery: the eccentrics, the patriots, the peasants, the epileptics, the sentimentalists and Tyrolese singers, singers of all kinds.

Diction: it was the turn of Mme Duparc, Mme Gilberte, Mme Thibaut, Mme Béliat, Mme. Tusini and the somewhat spindly Mlle Caudette, one of the summer starlets at the Café Alcazar.

The queens of the marchers: Mlle Levya and her "Volontaires" and "La tokinoise et les Parisiennes."

The eccentrics: Mme Demay (with "Oh, son Victor qui dort"), the formidable Mme Faure and Mme Bloch. But what sharp notes coming from Mme Amiati, what a patriot! Cover your ears when she begins to bellow her "Cuirassier de Reichshoffen," her "Stances à Hugo" or her "Hommage à Courbet".

The epileptic singers went for a particular kind of song. Mlle Violet sang "Le Tramway d'la Chapelle"; Mlle Heps sang "Le p'tit vin de Bercy"; and Mme Gilette sang "Le p'tit picton de Suresnes". In the sentimental bracket there was Mme Juana who simply wept. Meanwhile the mixed singers just sang whatever they could get hold of and the Tyrolese songs were crooned by the Bruet couple. Degas' studies of these women were sketches, not real portraits. One cannot forget the glorious Paula Brèbion and Mlle Bonnaire, the real triumph of the Concert Parisien. From here [Degas] went to the Scala, the Eldorado, to the Alcazar d'Hiver, to the Eden Concert, the Pépinière, the Ba-ta-Clan, the Époque au Ternes, the Belleville and the Villette. In summer he frequented the Horloge, the Ambassadeurs and the Alcazar d'Été.

The Degas that Paul Valéry got to know was not the same Degas he had had in mind as a model for Monsieur Teste: The idea I had acquired of Degas was of a character who was reduced by the rigors of painstaking research, a kind of Spartan, a stoic, a Jansenist artist. His main characteristic was a form of intellectual brutality. Shortly before I had written about an evening with Monsieur Teste. It was an imaginary portrait piece, though constructed from real notes and verifiable observations, which were influenced by the figure of Degas as I imagined him.

But he had the cogency of spirit that defined the fundamental traits of the man and his work. Valéry notes that Degas was sometimes likable, sometimes not.

He either had, or wished to appear to have, the worst character imaginable, and yet there were days of unpredictable warmth. On such occasions, he was entertaining and indulged in farcical behavior, became suddenly familiar like some impish apprentice or some odd character of Neapolitan extraction.

Showing a good eye for detail, Valéry described the man and his studio at No. 37, Rue Victor Massé: He received me in a long attic room with a wide window (rather dirty) at one end, a room full of light and dust. It was crammed with a toilet, a zinc bathtub, seedy dressing gowns, the little dancer girl with her dress of real organdie, a glass showcase, a row of easels displaying creatures drawn in carbon, busts, snubnosed girls, torsos, a girl drawing a comb through her thick hair, pulled tight with her other

Exterior of the Café Riche at the turn of the century.
(photo by R. Viollet)

Paris, Montmartre, c. 1900.
(Photo by A. Harlingue)

Paris, Alcazar in the summertime.
(photo by R. Viollet)

97

hand. *Along the window, gently lit by the sun, there was a narrow shelf loaded with boxes, flasks, pencils, sticks of pastel, blades and other useful objects.*

Degas had spread himself over three floors of the house. He used the top floor as his studio, the first for his large collection (Corot, Ingres) and the second for his home.

Once again, Valéry provides a vivid profile of the aging painter. *In his apartment on the second floor he has a large gloomy dining room where I have eaten several times. Degas was worried about getting an inflammation and a blocked intestine. The veal was tough and the macaroni very slowly served up by the old maid Zoe was wholly insipid. I had to eat my way through some Dundee jam, which I loathed but learned to cope with and even tolerate, sitting there opposite the old man steeped in lugubrious reveries, deprived (owing to his failing eyesight) of the work that was his very life. He would then offer me a cigarette as hard as nails and watched me as I softened the contents by rolling it between my fingers. Zoe brought the coffee, resting her belly against the table and speaking in clear tones–she was a teacher apparently. The thick eyeglasses she wears gave a cultured look to her wide, honest and eternally serious face.*

This glimpse of Degas is very revealing, a Degas whose eyesight was rapidly failing and whose work had become increasingly laborious. But the capricious painter had not yet lost his hiding-place, his oasis. A few years before his death, however, disaster struck. He received notice to evacuate his house, which was to make way for a block of apartments. *He was shattered. He tried to speak to the owner, used all the excuses he could about his health. There was nothing doing, the storm was approaching, threateningly. Within a few months it was upon him and he was forced to leave. He was unable to work. Where before he would sit in his "lair" and rarely venture out, now he began to stay out again, wrapped in melancholy, dropping in on a few friends, passing from one to the other in search of comfort and a reason to go on living. His fellow café-goers of the* days of the Guerbois no longer appealed to him: he had nothing more to say to Renoir and Monet. He began to visit Bartholomé again and frequent his younger friends, Suzanne Valadon and Zuloaga[1].

And it was Valadon who found a new studio for Degas (it was to be his last) in No. 6, Boulevard Clichy. It was a large studio, previously occupied by a painter of historical scenes. As it was not far from Rue Victor Massé, Degas was able to continue with his old routines – his walks from the Boulevard to Place Clichy, Place Blanche and Place Pigalle, Place d'Anvers and Boulevard Rochechouart; his cafés – the Ermitage, the Nouvelle Athènes, the Rat Mort; his theaters – the Montmartre and the Batignolles.

The older he got, the more Degas became morose and vindictive, like some ancient Oedipus tottering through the crowd, muttering insults and anathemas. *Once he had become old and almost blind, he showed horror for the cyclists, for bus and car drivers. Every time he went out he swore he would do away with them all.*

It was certainly a pathetic way to end. Gustave Coquiot paints a last cruel picture of the old man as he wandered about the city, helpless: *He was never more full of hate and bitterness than now. A book could be filled with his outbursts. Everyone avoided him and he was afraid of dying. He would repeat to himself the words "beyond the grave" with desperate emphasis. They would take him to the Café Victor at the corner of Rue Batignolles and sat him at a table. When he got up to leave, I watched his heavy cloak-overcoat, limp hat and large umbrella, crudely closed, knocking against the curbstone as he moved off.*

Almost blind and eternally irritable, Degas lost none of the characteristics that had always distinguished him. According to Suzanne Valadon, when he was almost seventy, he was still a handsome man. "He had Verlaine's forehead, a fine mouth and his agate eyes were still full of irony", she wrote.

A photograph made by Bartholomé in his garden

Degas in his garden.
(Photo courtesy Bibliothèque Nationale)

Degas – Standing in front of his house.
(Photo courtesy Bibliothèque Nationale)

At the Races. (1877-80)
Paris, Louvre.
Degas captured the intensity of real moments through his choice of framing.

La Villette - St-Sulpice Omnibus.
(photo by R. Viollet)

shows Degas with a straggly gray beard and long bushy hair. His features are drawn and sad. *One day in 1917, amidst the general alarm caused by the air attacks and cannon-fire closing in on Paris, Degas passed away quietly in his sleep. His death had little effect on a public that was fraught by the deaths of thousands of young men on all sides[2].*

He was buried in the cemetery at Montmartre on September 29. Thirty people or more attended the funeral, including Jean Béraud, Bonnat and Forain. Degas had told them not to make any speeches, but added that if Forain were to say anything, then let him say that "he liked drawing".

(1) Gustave Coquiot.
(2) Georges Rivière.

THE MORALIST

One of the more conventional ways to trace the evolution of painting in the 19th century is to study the changes that occur in the landscape as the relationship between the painter and the environment altered over the decades. The change brought about a considerable widening of the visual horizon, to the point where the painter was no longer depicting the particular section before him but nature itself in a global sense, i.e. not nature as seen, but nature as a lived space. Similarly, the evolution of the portrait was greatly affected by the introduction of photography in the 19th century. The portrait too experienced deep changes. It ceased to be a precise account of a mere fragment of the visual world and became instead the product of the sensibilities of the painter. The artist was felt to act as a filter for the nature he sees, crystallizing his own perception of the world. In the case of the portrait, the artist gradually came to replace the subject's real features with his personal concept of them.

Degas arrived just when the standard 18th-century practice of painting a man in his professional or noble apparel, with a "faithful" portrayal of his facial features, was giving way to a more inventive approach. The new conception involved first assimilating the psychology of the subject.

The "psychological" portrait was really Goya's invention. Under the guise of Classical form, he performed a lasting transformation of the pictorial vision. *In comparison with the great contemporary portrait paintings, those of Goya appear to be classical compositions in which the background and furnishings are non-existent or are reduced to a minimum. But the lack of balance between the foreground figure and the background (which was an established formula of the 18th century, originally defined by Anthony van Dyck) is not the real originality of these works. Goya rejected the principle of balancing the various parts of the composition, and instead deliberately made the subject stand out from the setting, isolating the figure by means of the illumination. In this way, the personality, gesture or pose* and even lineaments of the subject were highlighted.

Degas followed these guidelines, keen to underscore the interior values of his subjects and not be side-tracked by the details of the setting. He did, however, often create "portraits" in which the setting was deliberately indicative of the subjects, as in *The Belleli Family* and *The Viscomte Lepic*. Here, the details are not included so much to highlight the subjects, but to emphasize the relationship these people had with their home environment. Both canvases represent Degas' incursion into daily life rather than any particular social issues, and the subjects were people Degas was in a position to observe at close range. Apart from the psychological slant, these studies were a prelude for certain purely plastic approaches Degas was to explore in later portraits of families, dancers and nudes. Sometimes the arrangement of the figures was unusual or the viewing angle was diagonal (as in *Absinthe*). At others the scene seemed to be one of a series, a still from a film, a freeze-frame from a narrative.

These investigations led Degas to a genre he was to completely revolutionize, focusing on *a component that was vital to later developments in painting. The intrinsic value of the composition was greater than that of the subject and the representation of the layout in the traditional sense*[1].

Degas strove for increasingly pictorial solutions to his ideas, without however overlooking the literary angle he sought, especially in his portraits. Both Degas and Manet felt that portraits were a means for communicating the same psychological profile found in the contemporary novel. Francastel noted in the works of Guy de Maupassant: *Through the works of Manet and Degas, the bourgeois novel insinuates its way into painting through the portrait, set in an atmosphere that is more Maurasian than Balzacian in character.*

Where did Degas find his models? For his nudes, he used prostitutes, who were merely bodies to him. His dancers were just legs and arms caught in a dizzy balance, usually in a precarious environment.

For his portraits he turned to members of the family – aunts, brothers, sisters, the Montejaci-Cicereale family, the Belleli or friends like the Valpinçons, Rouart, Dihau, Diego Martelli, Duranty, Mary Cassatt and Bonnat.

"They are pretexts", said Degas. Even in times of financial difficulty, unlike Renoir, he was able to choose his models freely and the way he represented them.

Georges Hilaire explains what Degas was trying to prove: *"By freeing his painting from conventional formulas and artificial touches, reducing the technical means to a minimum, Degas was able to capture the austerity behind the family dignity (see* The Belleli Family*) fixed and transcended in this translation to the canvas. The appeal of his work stems less from the strange anecdotal and "moral" projection of the contents, which was not in itself new to painting (e.g. Francisco de Zurbaran, Philippe de Champaigne), than from the sheer incisiveness of the execution.*

(1) Pierre Francastel. *Le Portrait*.

MOVEMENT AS SUBJECT MATTER

Between 1866, when he presented his picture of a horse-race to the Salon, and 1874, the year of the first Impressionist Exhibition, which offered the full range of his theme material, Degas concentrated on two particular subjects that appealed to him for the same basic reason. Horse-races and ballerinas were two aspects of the same challenge that was fundamental to any artist determined to live his epoch to the full. Degas tackled the challenge without Manet's force, but by a process of deduction, a system of logic and rationale. Degas perceived strong links between the horse, which he termed "magnificently nude in its silk covering," and the ballerina, "whose satin feet embroider such pleasing designs." For Degas they were two expressions or aspects of movement, his central preoccupation. This subject brought him back time and time again to the race-track and backstage at the ballet. In 1860, while Degas was staying at the home of his friends the Valpinçons, which was situated near a stud farm, he made his first paintings of horses. There was a certain coherence in his attraction to both horses and dancers: *Horses also walk on their toes. Only a thoroughbred has the perfect poise of a ballerina in movement. The hand of the horse's rider seems to hold it up as it breaks into a trot in the sunshine*[1].

Pictures like *The Gentlemen's Race* and *Steeple Chase Scene* are revealing examples of how far ahead Degas was in his research into the subject. He soon came across the writings of Major Muybridge who pointed out the errors of painters and sculptors who depicted racehorses.

Degas was fascinated by photography, which he diligently studied, gaining a great many valuable insights on realism. The inexpert handling we find in the first canvases on dancers is repeated in his early attempts at painting horses. *The Ballet Hall at L'Opéra Rue le Peletier* is considered a masterpiece, and yet it is only the first of a series of works devoted to the world of dance. Degas borrowed the receding perspectives from the Dutch masters, using open doors and mirrors, arranging the figures so that the

Racehorses Before the Stands.
Paris, Louvre.

Gentlemen's Race.
Paris, Louvre.

Horses at the Races. (1873-75)
Boston, Museum of Fine Art.
A reporter's eye.

Horses – sculptures.
Paris, Louvre.

a. Rearing up.
b. Standing.
c. Taking off to clear an obstacle.
d. Galloping.

center of the painting is practically empty and the viewer's attention is drawn to the chair in the foreground. The figures themselves are perhaps still rather static, but this was to change, as they began to express pure movement. This is one of the many aspects that brought his work close to that of the Impressionists. Degas stuck with them, sharing their joys and disappointments. And like them, he too would be dumbfounded by the vacuousness of the critics, inuring himself to the ridicule of a public that failed, dismally, to appreciate the new art being born in its midst, of which it was necessarily a part.

Degas would not, however, give his support to any new expression that was not based on proper values. Indeed, his own inventions and innovations were firmly based on a legacy that was almost a straitjacket to him.

The word "impression" came about for lack of a better term to describe the work of this new crop of artists, to which Degas and his strictly visual techniques were irreversibly linked. In the same way as the artists of Monet's school were bent on catching the fleeting interplay of light, Degas attempted to capture the essence of movement, the intricacies of bodily posture and gesture.

Unlike the Impressionists, who worked and reworked the light to the point of dematerializing form itself, Degas took a more constructive path as he was essentially interested in the body, in something more specific and defined. Due to this irreversible logic, his inquiry into painting led him to try his hand at sculpture.

According to his brother Bartholomé, Degas had actually experimented with this medium in 1870, with a bas-relief entitled *Young Women Picking Apples*, a theme suggested by Renoir[2]. Speaking of the work, Renoir told Ambroise Vollard that he considered Degas greater even than Rodin. His research into movement and his nagging eye trouble induced Degas to branch out in his spatial investigations as he got older. At the 1881 Impressionist Exhibition, Degas presented *Little Ballerina of*

Fourteen. This was the only sculpture he ever made public during his life, as he considered them all research pieces only. The series of horses and ballerinas signal a highly original grasp of space and movement that goes far beyond any mere stylistic investigation. Pierre Cabanne is right to speak of Degas as having "an extra eye" in his open-minded approach to sculpture. The pieces show amazing boldness and mark the start of a new idiom.

Not satisfied with his two main themes, Degas then set to work on sculpture portraits. He began on one of his friend Zandomeneghi, who had died earlier, and one of the Valpinçon daughters.

Degas mentioned them in a letter to Bartholomé: *If you want to know why I am still here, I'll tell you. "How come you don't paint anything of Hortense?" her mother asked me. What do they expect me to do? I set to work on a large bust made of clay and gravel. The family is following my work with a mixture of curiosity and commotion. There is no fun in these things unless there is something off-center, like me. It is not too bad, except for my legs, which are sunk into the trunk and my arms which have tired. Toward the weekend I am returning to Paris and after this stint at "earning my bread" I shall be off to Normandy again to check up on the reproduction of the piece. The family members look on, clad in their Norman peasant costumes, their faces full of doubt, but very glad in their hearts.*

He was obviously very gratified by this work, as he even spoke to Ludovic Halévy about it: *They are keeping me here til the end of the week – or I am just staying on – so as to get this bust with arms finished. It is taking some time, but I am enjoying it. The interest it has aroused almost verges on wicked curiosity. This is why I have opted for making a good likeness, or something even more perhaps.*

He also wrote to Henri Rouart: *What a muddle I have got myself into. We know so little about what we do the moment we cease to let ourselves be steered by our profession. They say that open-mindedness will help you achieve anything. That may be so, but what a confounded muddle it is!*

There is therefore a common intention behind the paintings of the races, the ballerinas and the sculptures Degas made "in private", which also focused on the same two themes (except for the busts mentioned here).

Furthermore, the viewing angle of both race and ballerina paintings was chosen to instill the canvas with a sense of movement.

When Degas paints a plane of color behind his main subject (highlighting areas of canvas to complement the foreground action), it is not to provide decoration, as Gauguin would, but to contrast the features of the setting (the race-track, or the effect of light on the furniture in the ballet scenes) and bring out the turbulence of the foreground movement against the simplicity and evenness of the painting's general tone[3].

Degas always sought to use new and untried compositions for his paintings of ballerinas.

When applied to the paintings centered on musical themes, this skill in arranging his subject matter, this spatial mobility, led Degas toward an increasingly virtuoso expression.

Before the war in 1870, Degas met Désiré Dihau, who lived in the same part of the city. The artist was a great admirer of the shows at the Opèra and often went with his friend to the Café Rochefoucauld where he was allowed to go behind the scenes.

In fact, Degas *became good friends with many from Dihau's company, invited them to his father's house for the Monday evening meeting with the warmth typical of the times. Among the group was Mme. Camus the pianist and her husband; Manet (who often sat cross-legged on the floor in front of the fireplace) and his wife who was also a musician; Mme. Dihau, a talented singer whom Degas' father had sought out in Rue Taitbout at the house of friends where she used to dine and who came back to Rue Laval with her brother Désiré and their neighbor Degas; finally there was the bucolic Pangas. It was Pangas that Degas painted a small portrait of playing a guitar, with the artist's father in the background*

Ballerinas – sculptures.
Paris, Louvre.

a. Looking at her toes.
b. Grande Arabesque, third phase.
c. Grande Arabesque, second phase.

The Wait. (1882)
New York, Havemeyer Collection.
Realistic even in his interpretation of an insignificant moment. A picture
that is worth a thousand words.

Spanish Dancer - sculpture.
Paris, Louvre.

The Wait. (1882)
New York, Havemeyer Collection.
Realistic even in his interpretation of an insignificant moment. A picture
that is worth a thousand words.

sitting at the piano, his hands hanging down and a pensive look on his face.

But Degas was interested in the form of the instruments too. Their plasticity and expressive shape fascinated him. He decided to capture it all on paper, and made a series of drawings of *the twisting of the hand, the arm and neck of the violinist, the puffing in and out of the cheeks of the oboe-player, etc.*

He did many works on this theme, depicting the various aspects of music through portraits of his friends, such as Pillet (cello), Gouffé (double bass), Dihau (bassoon), Altès (flute) and Goût (violin). Then, after this series of individual portraits, he painted the larger works including the entire orchestra of the Opéra: *Degas made a bold move when he turned all his attention on this complex, which usually goes unnoticed. He suddenly made the delightful discovery of the effects of artificial lighting and changing colors, and made it his own special field of research. After studying the orchestra, he passed onto the stage itself and became absorbed in the sets[4].*

He would walk round his characters, choosing odd perspectives and adopting some highly original angles. In one of his notebooks, he sketched out some ideas: *Make simple operations such as sketching an immobile profile that then moves, rising and falling, a full figure, a piece of furniture, an entire drawing room. Draw a series of arm movements during a dance, or of a leg held still, moving round it. Study a figure from all possible viewpoints, an object, anything. Cut unsparingly. Draw the arms, legs and back of a ballerina; draw her shoes, the hands of the hairdresser, the clipped hair, naked feet in a dance pose.*

Oddly enough, some of the ideas in this list would not emerge until his later period of nudes. Meanwhile, Degas began to roam the theaters backstage, noting every detail, every attitude and pose, discovering completely novel images and untried viewpoints, as in the painting *Curtain*, so admired by

117

Ballerina in Fourth Position – sculpture.
Paris, Louvre.

The Ballet Lesson. (1874)
Paris, Louvre.

Huysmans: *I have traced out a pastel-colored theater curtain, an empty curtain bordering the set, with a half-raised cherry-red curtain and the background purple and a darker shade than the wallpaper. A woman in profile leans over the upper balcony looking down on the whimpering actors. Her face is flushed in the heat of the theater, the blood has risen to her cheeks and reddened her ears; the beam of light catching her is portrayed with great precision*[5].

Then Degas ventured into the wings, documenting the intriguing comings and goings of the seedy dressing rooms. *Ambling about the theater corridors, Degas spied a ballerina, through a half-open door of a dressing room, standing ready to go onstage; in another direction he saw another crudely lit up from below by the gaslight as she added the last touches to her hair; he watched how the dressers flounced the ballerinas' skirts, while an old man who haunted the corridors leant on his cane.*

There was never anything frivolous or lackadaisical in Degas' work, as he tried to grasp the workings of the human body. By studying the rapid, demanding movements of the dancers, he hoped to discover what it was that made the muscular stress so graceful and full of poise. Many of these compositions are peopled with ballerinas exercising at the bar. The chronology of the paintings on the subject confirms Degas' passion for movement and the gradual evolution of his vision. The early paintings tend to be rather static, but gradually he turned his attention to the figures' movement and had to modify his technique. Painting in oils was rather a hindrance. He needed a way of quickly capturing the movements he witnessed and so turned to pastels. The technique was not entirely new to him, but this time he appreciated their versatility, aware also of their basic fragility. He launched himself into a series of complicated studies, mixing pastel and gouache and tempera. The first trials were not always successful, as can be seen in the rather granular and patchy result of some canvases. Eventually, he chose to work with pastel tempera. This involved softening the

118

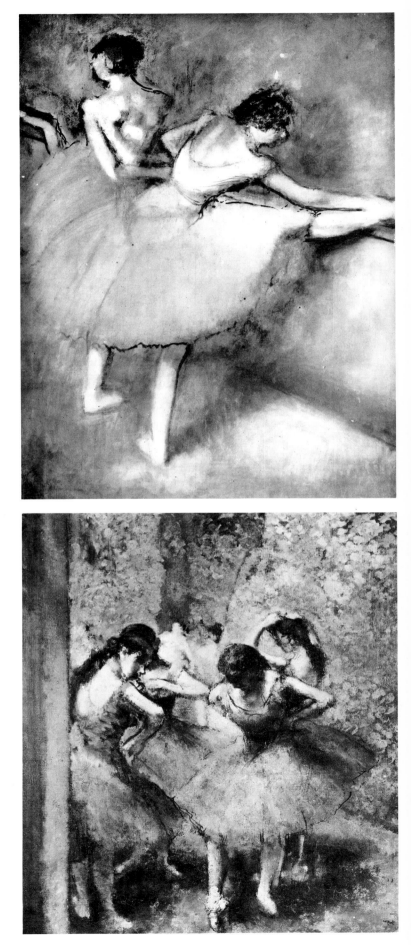

Ballerinas Getting Ready for the Ballet. (1878) Chicago, Art Institute.

Ballerinas Exercising at the Barre. (1884-88) Washington, D. C., The Phillips Collection.
...lively line that foreshadows Picasso in his blue period.

Blue Ballerinas. (1890) Paris, Louvre.

pastels in fixative and pasting it on in opaque layers, blurring the outlines and then finishing off the painting with smaller touches and details with pure pastels and sepia brushstrokes to give a pleasant fluid effect. *Ballerina with Bouguet, Taking her Bows* and *The Star* are the best examples of this technique. It is difficult to analyze and separate out the various reworkings Degas effected to the canvases, as he had a vast range of choices open to him and used them according to the effect he was looking for. His spontaneity increased as he got more acquainted with his materials and tools and the more he wanted to catch a gesture or a figure in mid-movement, just as he had perceived it. While in the Impressionist paintings movement is represented by the unevenness of the painted surface or a series of fine marks of the brush tip (which was to lead to "Pointillisme"), or a set of colored impressions, in Degas' work, the sense of movement was expressed in firm, confident outlines. Gauguin's technique was similar, albeit with a more lush and languid manner.

For the Impressionists, movement was a sensation. In Degas it was a naturalistic expression. His insistence on more intimate motifs gave way to straightforward acceptance of the natural features of what he saw. It is one of the paradoxes of art: just as Degas seemed to be getting closer to reality, he began to express more what he felt inside, the things he perceived arbitrarily, without any real connections with the motifs of the object he was observing. As his vision began to transcend reality, Degas was heading for a world of abstraction.

Raymond Cogniat noted that *Degas belongs among the Impressionists, not because of his technique, but because of his basic inner disposition and his utter rejection of the conventional world. His training had taught him the most sophisticated techniques, and the spectacle of reality itself gave him a sense of life. From this point of view Degas intuited the vast possibilities the real world offered him, beyond anything his friends were actually doing.*

Dress Rehearsal of a Ballet. (1873-75)
Paris, Louvre.
Degas frequently returned to this theme, in this work with great precision
and a fine "black and white" effect.

The Ballet Hall at L'Opéra, Rue le Peletier, or *The Dance Examination*.
(1872)
Paris, Louvre.
In a single, continuous composition, the painter studies the unfolding of
the ballerinas' movements, the variety of their positions and their
gestures.

Degas

The Cellist Pillet. (1868+69)
Paris, Louvre.
This shifted perspective is typical of the painter's work.

House at the Foot of a Cliff. (1895-98)
One of a series depicting Saint-Valéry-sur-Somme.

Miss Lola at the Cirque Fernando. (1879)
London, National Gallery.
A gripping, cinematographic perspective.

The Opéra Orchestra. (1868-69)
Paris, Louvre.
Identifiable figures in this work include composer Ernest Chabrier, cellist Pillet, flautist Altes, as well as Pagans, close friend of the Degas family, who already appeared in a portrait of the artist's father.

By choosing movement as the fulcrum of his art, Degas was several decades ahead of his time and anticipated an area of contemporary art that would gradually substitute representation for movement. Without anticipating what in those days was only a pictorial problem, Degas managed to capture the essence of something that would later become the research of the Futurists, who called for the destruction of matter and thereby superseded the forms of representation that Degas himself could not forego, given his cultural foundations. Degas did his utmost to emulate Ingres and followed the latter's advice about being able "to paint a man falling from the roof." But to paint the fall did not mean omitting the object, the falling body itself.

This would come later, with Cubism and Marcel Duchamp who broke up his figure into an infinite number of cells (*Nude Descending a Staircase*), replacing the figure with a trace of its transition. Without straying outside the bounds of painting, Degas reasoned with the mind of a sculptor. The Impressionists, on the other hand, committed to the effects of color, prepared the way for the suppression of forms themselves. Today, painting has reached the point in which it makes do with reflecting gestures, of which it has become the immobile and passive witness.

(1) Paul Valéry.
(2) Reported by Ambroise Vollard.
(3) Georges Hilaire.
(4) P.A. Lemoisne.
(5) Exposition des Indépendants. *L'Art Moderne* 1880.

THE LANDSCAPE STYLE

After centuries of serving merely as a scenic back-drop, in the 19th century the countryside and land-scape became central themes of painting. The mythological painters of the previous century were replaced by a squadron of painters who engaged in a head-on confrontation with nature in its most immediate form. The emphasis had shifted. The new subject was the landscape itself, without human figures, a landscape cleansed of action and seen for its geography, its atmospherical conditions, its perennial beauty. The logical painter was supplanted by the emotive painter. It was a moment of spiritual decadence, but it signaled the arrival of all those who were moved by nature, by the winter silence of meditations on the lake. The first landscape artists began to describe what they felt and saw, sometimes with extraordinary command, knowing that the truth they sought was there in what they saw. Almost contemporary with the Impressionists, a painter appeared on the scene who was pursuing a synthesis of the glorious spectacle of nature and the need for inner order. He would replace the visual dilution of the Impressionists with a new vision of construction. He discarded emotive content in favor of reflection. The artist was Paul Cézanne and his art created an indelible bridge linking the work of the 17th-century artist Gaspard Poussin with that of Georges Braque.

The revolution accomplished by Edgar Degas was perhaps less evident than those being achieved in other fields, but no less radical.

Degas' interiors and portraits reveal him to be a soul-searcher, an acute observer of the human dilemma. Unlike his Impressionist friends, Degas was unable to tackle the "landscape" on the same plane as his interiors. *While Monet was set on exploring the universe of light, Degas concentrated his energies on studying the psychology of forms and of certain "products" of modern civilization*[1].

But he by no means wished to be categorized as an "open-air" artist and recommended the firing squad to those artists who set up their easels in front of their subject.

133

At the Seaside. Nanny Combing Little Girl's Hair. (1874-77)
London, National Gallery.
A masterful use of light in the superimposition of the gestures over a natural backdrop. Unlike the Impressionists, who worked on the atmosphere, Degas focused on gestures outlined in broad arabesques.

Of his Impressionist friends, Degas declared: *They need a natural life, I need an artificial one.*

The mistake of the Impressionists is that they wanted to portray the air itself, the air we breathe. But the air we see in the paintings of the great masters is not air one can breathe.

Despite the wry tone of his remark, it contains an important truth. During his stay in Normandy, Degas painted a few landscapes, in Boulogne, then in Trouville alongside his friend Manet in 1869-1870 and in Saint-Valéry en Caux.

Degas' unerring gaze caught the typical aspects of the place, the grayish greens of the sea with its fringe of silver along the beach, the curving sand, the heavy line of hills, the velvety green of a meadow or the shifting lacework of the clouds.

His observations are unusually beautiful, full of elusive colors and mother-of-pearl tones, allowing us only a fine skeleton of what he really saw, revealing only the essential force lines.

The artist preceded even Cézanne in creating a synthesis of his vision. His perception of detail was almost incidental, preferring to capture the general "feel" or interior life of the subject matter.

While they appear modern in approach, Degas' rare landscapes tend to rely on memory more than real observation. They are like a set of quick notes and for this reason they seem to come close to the Impressionist landscapes. Actually, they are re-lived images, passed carefully through the filter of memory. While he was staying with Degas on his tour through the Bourgogne in 1890, Jeanniot had occasion to observe how Degas was able to draw on his prodigious memory and practically "see" the details of the various landscapes they had passed through: *And yet, he never stopped to pay any particular attention to anything.*

Once he had the right equipment about him, he went straight into his work. With his strong, well-shaped fingers, he gripped the things he needed with a strange coarseness. Gradually, on the surface of the metal we began to see first a valley, then the sky, some white houses, fruit trees with dark branches, birches and chestnut trees, lanes filled with the recent rain, thunderclouds looming in a sky like a canopy over the red and green land.

Everything was ordered, linked together, the tones melded well and the paintbrush traced out the clear forms in the fresh paint. These fine things just appeared without any apparent effort, as if he had the scene in front of him. Bartholomé recognized the places they had been to, including the gait of the white horse. Once the first proofs were printed, they were hung up to dry. He did about three or four each morning. Then he asked for some pastels to complete the Monotypes and in that very moment I admired his taste and judgment even more than when he was doing the proof, his imagination and the vivid freshness of his memories. He remembered the variety of the forms, the contours of the land, the unexpected clashes of opposites and contrasts. It was marvelous.

The intuitiveness of his powers of observation can be seen in every stage of his works, his desire to convey his vision in the most essential line imaginable (the line of a body or a line that lends structure) was in fact in tone with the artistic preoccupations of the times. One of the main preoccupations of the Impressionists was in fact to capture the sense of passing time. Later, Cézanne would achieve an expression of fundamental unity in his art. Degas' painting was no more descriptive than Monet's, nor more analytical than Cézanne's. Degas paid more attention than Cézanne to the atmosphere of the moment, but attempted to express a lastingness that Monet, who wanted to capture only a fleeting moment, could never express. Degas managed to answer the challenge and successfully united the contrasts, merging these contrasting intentions.

(1) Gustave Geffroy. *Histoire de l'Impressionnisme.*

THE LUBRICIOUS ANIMALS

Nothing is known of Degas' relationships with women. His bounding affection for Mary Cassatt was mainly due to his great admiration for her work. Later on, Toulouse-Lautrec would introduce him to the infamous Suzanne Valadon, whose large but soft features attracted him. There was a certain Maria, who turned down his somewhat frequent written invitations to visit him. Much later, when Florent Fels asked the woman if she had been Degas' lover, she replied: *Never! He was too timid. His admiration was purely material – he was drawn by my acrobat's body. But my greatest satisfaction was when he asked me to make him a present of one of my drawings[1].*

This is confirmed by one of Degas' notes, reproduced by Lemoisnes: *Dear Maria, your letter reached me punctually, as usual, with your self-confident handwriting. But where are your drawings? Now and then I gaze across the dinner table at your red crayon drawing and I say to myself: that devil of a woman Maria certainly had a genius for drawing!*

We can assume that Degas was more fascinated by Valadon's solid beauty, as she herself acknowledged. Hers was the rough beauty of the prostitutes Degas used for his nudes. Degas' knowledge of women was really limited to the models who came to his studio, and at times he somewhat longingly compared his own life with that of his brothers, who had each settled into family life. *He saw his brothers and his friends set up home and enjoy the joys and worries of creating a family. He was tempted to establish stronger ties, but realized that his work would have been hindered by the many obligations that would result from such a move. Meanwhile, here among his brothers and his friends, Degas betrayed an intense capacity for affection that he jealously kept from the eyes of those who did not know him[2].*

Generally speaking, there is nothing cruel in Degas' treatment of his women. They are left to themselves, depicted busy looking after their bodies. His figures are a far cry from the elegant sweetness of Pierre Bonnard's mother-of-pearl nymphs. Nor do they resemble the weird and won-

135

derful females of Rouault. And yet there is something decidedly savage in the quick sketches Degas did for Ambroise Vollard for his illustrations of Guy de Maupassant's *Maison Tellier*. One can detect the restrained loathing of a misogynist wandering through this "sexual inferno." Corpulent matrons, "Venuses of the gutter," lolling about, their hair piled up on their heads, unashamedly exposing themselves. Hardly the luxurious perfumed havens of Baudelaire's verbal palette, with the "dim light of languid lamps falling on soft perfumed cushions". Degas' woman was a kind of female satyr, diabolical and outrageous like something from a Fellini film, bizarre, malicious, impetuous, set in an atmosphere that reeked of closed rooms lacking any contact with the real world, closer to death than life. Degas was a kind of Léon Bloy of the painting world, vilifying women. On the whole, unlike Renoir and his bloated sensuality and Manet's mother-of-pearl glorification of the female flesh, Degas' vision was curiously objective. That is how he wanted to be. One day, he confided "Perhaps I have always considered woman as a sort of animal"[3]. This observation lends a certain logic to his three interconnected central themes: the races, ballerinas and women *à la toilette*. On the other hand, it emphasizes the objective distance achieved by an artist who considered his subject matter solely as a means for obtaining a certain kind of plasticity.

Unlike Ingres, he did not pursue the lines of the body to the point of idealizing them. He bore in mind that "flesh is mud transformed into gold by light". And like Rembrandt, Degas *accepted what he saw, accepted women for what they were. He only found fat or thin women, and the few beautiful ones he did find he chose for their particular spark of vivaciousness rather than for their outward form. He was not put off by the corrugated, rolling flaccidity of fat bellies, ungainly limbs, reddened clumsy hands, common-looking features. He managed to impregnate these backs, bellies, breasts and mounds of flesh, those ugly creatures and servant girls, with a kind of sunlight that was all his own, mixing reality with something mysterious, "animalesque" and even divine[4].*

Degas had a streak of voyeurism. Thoroughly embittered though not wanton, he handled his women engrossed in their personal care with an almost embarrassing familiarity. He was trying to bring these women to life, to deliver them from the realm of his imagination. In place of Bouguereau's cloyingly angelic visions of women, Degas proposed a grim and scrupulous realism: *The human beast busy cleaning itself, the cat licking itself. Until now, the nude was presented to an imaginary audience. My women are simple, candid women absorbed in their physical activities. Here is one washing her feet: it is as if you were looking at her through the keyhole.*

As his eyesight became increasingly feeble, Degas began to achieve something that had been out of reach when he was younger and still under the influence of Ingres. He managed to capture what was real not through intelligence of reflection, but through emotion. The artist who swore he would "put a spell on truth and give it the appearance of madness," was a stickler for rules. Almost blind and nearing the end of his days, Degas finally reached this lyrical intimacy, which had been denied him owing to his commitment to form.

Through the body, he reached the reality he had always sought after. His contemporaries misunderstood his new intuition and thought his work was gratuitously unwholesome and smacked of cheap eroticism.

Even Huysmans, who had always applauded the artist's work, declared that Degas had *committed an outrage to the century he lived in by desecrating his idol, woman – by showing her at her bath, but now he had trespassed on her innermost intimacy.*

Through this fixation, we can trace Degas' development from 1880 – with his absolute fascination with light and simple finery such as interiors, objects and fabrics – as he passes on to an absorption in flesh (as in *La Toilette* and *The Bath*) and thence,

now almost blind, to a passion for mere sections of the body, which he paints with vehemence.

He worked the canvas with large movements, paying more attention to volume in its broadest sense and less to gesture (as in *Crouching Bather* and *La Toilette*). According to Valéry *Degas is searching for a single line that will express a given moment in the movement of a body, something exactingly precise but at the same time lavish.*

By degrees, this line gave solidity to mass and bore monuments of flesh that imposed themselves on the surface of the canvas. His progressive blindness brought him ever closer to the object he was painting and his pictorial vision was transformed into a sculptural one. By the same token, his sensuality gave way to anguish and even rage.

But as the man aged and found himself increasingly distanced from his female subject matter, relegated to the verge of desperation, he painted their flesh all the more vibrant. A flesh that was no longer sensual nor beautiful nor perturbing, as if he had made total acquaintance with it and it had no more effect on him. It had become a disquieting presence, a crushing mass, a stifled cry. Perhaps Degas' work heralded the contemporary vision called *new figuration* which, venturing beyond the marked lyrical emphasis of matter, had used its gestural content to discover an immobility, emerging from the shadows, the presence of the unconscious of the physical body.

(1) Quoted in Florent Fels. *L'Art et l'amour.* Arc en Ciel, 1953.
(2) As noted by Jean Nepveu-Degas, reproduced in Pierre Cabanne.
(3) Quoted in Georges Grappe. *Degas.*
(4) Quoted by Paul Valéry.

A BIASED WITNESS

Was Degas a realist? His critics are divided on the matter. In a letter to Georges Grappe, Bergson gives an interesting slant to this claim to realism: *I think you have fully grasped the essence and have made a thorough investigation of this artist who was a true realist, unlike those who claim to be realists, but merely strip reality bare.*

Another critic, François Fosca admits that: *More surprised and intrigued by the novelty of his subjects than by the rare power or originality of his art, the critics and dilettantes who studied his paintings saw him as a chronicler of the customs of modern Paris, an observer who complemented the incisive spirit of a backstage habitué with the disillusioned insights of the naturalist novelists.*

In their eyes, Degas occupied the same position in painting that Zola, Edmond de Goncourt, Maupassant and Huysmans held in literature. Without acknowledging the real intentions behind Degas' art, and somewhat narrowing down its scope and importance, the public has generally kept to this impression over the years.

Fosca also felt that *while it is true that Degas knew how to draw the aspects of Parisian daily life with such singular perspicacity, what really obsessed him in his long and labored existence were eminently aesthetic problems – problems of form and composition to which, in later years when his eye trouble prohibited him from painting, he added the problem of color. Degas would not have become the great artist he was if he had not addressed these problems, which constitute the very foundations of painting.*

Gustave Coquiot had less admiration for Degas: *Degas began all his work in his studio, with a dispassionate, collected approach, relying exclusively on the traditional skills imparted to him. With unerring intuition and a steady hand, Toulouse-Lautrec completed his definitive, characteristically arabesque sketches on site. This was an acquired skill. Degas was too attached to his studio and to working from memory. When he lived right opposite the Bal Tabarin dance hall he boasted to me that he had*

*never once set foot inside. Seeing my astonishment
(as I considered him a painter of modern life) he confessed to me that it made no difference to him who
posed as a dancer, laundresses or café-concert singer.
In this he was somewhat presumptuous. This is why
he often had professional models pose for him,
dressed up as dancers. Worse still: once when he
wanted to draw some jockeys, he got some women
who were visiting him to mount the dummy horses he
kept in the studio. That is how far he is from observing nature! It is like going back to the times when
Italian models, both men and women, hung about
the Place Pigalle in the chance of being able to pose
for some painter from the Académie in the guise of
Father Anchise, the goddess Ceres, some southern
bandit or a pensive figure à la Léopold Robert.*

*He detested modern life, with its newfangled ideas
and inventions heralding change; he cursed the electric light, the motor car, the elevator (however slow
and safe) and should have painted pictures of a more
relaxed kind (despite Duranty and the heated discussion at the Café Guerbois), conventional drawings
executed within the four walls of his silent and
dreamy studio, tucked away from it all, in a cul-de-
sac like the studio of Jean-Paul Laurens, Rue
Cassini.*

Once, in 1874, Edmond de Goncourt asked himself who had managed to capture the soul of modern
life. After a visit to the artist's studio, he concluded
that it was indeed Degas, because only Degas had responded to the declaration Baudelaire made in
1845: that the truly modern man was the one who
knew how to squeeze the epic side out of today's life
and convey to us through color and composition
how great and poetic we are in our fancy ties and
patent leather boots.

Duranty, natural successor to Mérimée and one
of the most lucid art critics of his day, to whom
Degas suggested a few key ideas that the writer
would express in authoritative terms, advised
people to *leave behind the stylized human body with
its static, vase-like appearance and instead capture*

the common man in a frock-coat, as Degas captured
those in the corridors of the Opéra, the café-concerts,
the Bourse and the private salons.

Duranty was referring to Degas when he spoke of
*one who does not hesitate to paint his models in black
frock-coats and tall hats, umbrella in hand, and set
them (their backs turned and seen from above) in the
corner of the canvas[1].*

Was Degas the only modern painter of his time?
But while Manet was also a witness to his era, a
biting critic like old Daumier, Manet drew on his
subjects out of a lack of imagination (and Daumier
out of sensitivity), whereas Degas seems to main-
tain a colder stance and keep his distance. And
though Toulouse-Lautrec venerated Degas, he
turned to the Daumier legacy for his scorn of men
and women, stripping them to their very souls.

But while Toulouse-Lautrec preferred stereotyped characters, humanity in general, Daumier focused on the inner workings of the society he was
observing. Degas was wholly apolitical and kept any
hint of politics or his opinions from his work. His
opinions were changeable and when he did express
them, he was peremptory.

He was against Dreyfus and displayed great insolence and foolhardiness on this score. According to
Valéry: *At the slightest clue, he would see into some-
body, explode with rage and storm off, turning his
back on his adversary, forever. Old and intimate
friends were suddenly cut off in this manner, without
any chance of patching up their relationship.*

Perhaps underneath he was an idealist, he was a
"man of the world who scorned approbation; ignor-
ant of business and the appeal of profit, he judged
those in power as if there had been a time when
power was exercised with integrity and complete
purity". He was a humanist, enamored with style,
keen to conserve his dignity even in his outward
behavior and dress; the words he used to translate
his thoughts were always exuberant. He was the
kind of man who judged politics as if it were art. *He
dreamed of a man of the ideal State, a man of pure*

passions who, whatever the people or circumstances, maintained the same determined openness and principled approach that he observed in his art[2].

But Degas lacked realism just when he believed he had come across the very foundations of truth. Since he had managed to develop his art through his mind, he imagined that in politics one could decide between contrasting values, as one could in art.

His opinion of Clémenceau is indicative of his reasoning. Degas considered the man *strangely egoistic, a Jacobin, an absolute, an aristocrat, aloof, an arch mocker of all and sundry, a man without friends except Monet but with a circle of old faithfuls, he loved to strike dread in the hearts of men, but was also capable of loving a people, of taking a tough line for its own good; a man of pleasure, pride and risks[3].*

Degas began to entertain the lofty and naive idea that, if he were in power, the importance of his position would dominate his thinking, that he would begin to lead an ascetic life, living in a modest apartment to which he would return straight from the Ministry each evening.

Valéry asked Degas what Clémenceau's reaction had been to all this. "He shot me a look of disgust". The next time Degas came across Clémenceau at the Opéra, he told him he had been to the House that very day.

"Throughout the entire meeting", he said, "I was unable to take my eyes off the door. I was convinced that at any minute that Danubian farmer would come in through that door. 'Now, now, Monsieur Degas', responded Clémenceau, 'we would never have let him get a word in'."[4]

Beneath Degas' somewhat puerile idealism lay a markedly unreal vision of the world. A vision that was more tuned to his own thinking and his problems than to the era in which he lived. For this reason, it was less his political ideals than a stance on aesthetics that made Degas so unobjective a witness.

What exactly was he looking for amid this modern world of racecourses, fashion boutiques, dance-halls and ballet schools? *Daumier painted the world of the street jugglers, while Degas preferred the café-concerts. Daumier was attracted to the Paris suburbs, to sideshows set up in the street or the rolling of a drum. Degas was fascinated by the ballet school during an examination, the murmuring of violins, the female form, the Parisian nudes caught in countless different attitudes. This was Degas[5].*

Such differences were also due to their habits. While Daumier roamed the streets, Degas kept strictly to his own social circles. Consequently, he was accused of being a painter of "high society". Coming between the romanticism of Daumier and the decadent impudence of Toulouse-Lautrec, Degas' wholly modern vision remained well within the bounds of respectability. Daumier's Paris is a phantasmagorical city, an awesome cruel place resembling those described by Hugo, Balzac and Dickens – a city of misery, hunger, cholera and fear. Degas' tone was always measured, sensible, even in the most modest manifestations of his art (e. g., *The Laundresses*).

There is no hint of revolt in his women's gestures. They are pictured going about their work, though their suffering is admitted, laid bare. Where Ingres delights in odalisks, Degas presents the woman of the street, women *à la toilette*. Instead of Delacroix's mythological females, we have Degas' woman factory worker. Perhaps Degas was more realist than is generally supposed, given his concerted research into plasticity. The woman yawning while her neighbor presses down hard on her iron, and another bent under the weight of her laundry basket – these are all women in movement. They are all purely formal observations that attracted the artist for their originality in terms of representation. Tired of the Olympian gods and goddesses of the Institut, Degas went in search of subjects from his own era, showing them in movement. In this, he was eminently coherent to his ideas. He is perhaps no more realist (and therefore a less impartial witness) than his friend Stéphane Mallarmé, who had styled

the Stock Exchange. (1876)
aris, Louvre.
he artist often liked to peer behind the stage of modern life.

Women Ironing. (1884)
Paris, Louvre.
Degas returned to this theme several times. It became a cliché of his
brand of populism.

his own form of realism in verse. Paul Valéry tells of one occasion when Degas was dining at Berthe Morisot's house with Mallarmé, and he was utterly engrossed in the intricacies of poetry:

He complained about the great difficulties af composing in verse: *What a dreadful vocation! I spent a whole day battling with a sonnet without getting anywhere. And yet I am full of ideas, too full in fact!*

My dear Degas, said Mallarmé with great tenderness, One does not write Poems with ideas, but with words.

Words and forms – expressions that were once based on myths and legends – were now firmly grounded in the real world. And the real world was now at the service of art.

(1) Georges Hilaire.
(2) Paul Valéry.
(3) *Ibid.*
(4) Georges Hilaire.
(5) Jaromir Pecirka. *Degas, dessins.* Cercle d'Art.

Degas was a realist of striking originality. While his contemporaries enthused about their new fictitious freedom with tangible reality, Degas managed to imagine, to *invent*, a reality that is in some ways linked to the birth of photography. Proust said that the photographer was a kind of Wandering Jew of the image, always searching for a different view of something already well-known. After a hesitant start due to the limitations of the standard layout of painting, photography really only came into its own with the advent of cinema. The camera became a tool for reading and transcribing the real world, a tool that went beyond reality itself, borrowing from it, upsetting the apparent order of things to find the secret rhythms, the essential components of the world, fixing its fleetingness on the canvas, the postures, glances and expressions of humankind.

Thirty years before the invention of cinema, Degas had anticipated its main characteristics in the flexibility of his planes and the relationships between them, the mobility of space and the simultaneity of images. *It is not fanciful to see in Degas' particular choice of composition and vantage point some of the techniques that would later be used in photography and cinema. His overhead "shots", his way of shifting the subject of a portrait to one side, of giving priority to the foreground, of accentuating an accessory object to emphasize the expression on someone's face – all these inventions coincide with the vision offered us today by the camera lens*[1].

Jean Cocteau also remarked on this interest of Degas' for photography. *I know that Degas sometimes blew up a photograph and then began working on it with his pastels, amazed at the potential of the composition, the unusual view and the distortion of the foreground*[2].

Germain Bazin pointed out that Degas *made the transition from the standard Renaissance perspective in three dimensions, to the multi-dimensional perspective of cinema. His spaces were no longer confined to a cube, just as a film director is able to shoot from various angles and later edit his shots.*

Carriage at the Races. (1870-73)
Boston, Museum of Fine Art.
A group portrait of Degas' friends (the Valpinçons) in one of the artist's
favorite settings, the racecourse.

Curtainfall. (1880)
Boston, Metcalf Collection.
Another clever framing device, so dear to Degas.

153

At the Milliner's. (1883)
New York, Metropolitan Museum.
A slice of Parisian life.

Degas portrayed the same action various times as it unfolded. In *Ballerina Holding Her Foot* and *Ballerina with Raised Arm*, to convey the instability of the moment's action Degas set the picture off-balance, making the composition eccentric, just as a photographer would position a figure in a corner or the background, ready to bring it into view. Furthermore, as with cinema, the realism of Degas became a mental representation of reality. As with a film director, Degas did much more than choose a corner of the world and observe it: in some way he *imagined* it, starting with the essential.

His is not an objective transcription of nature as it stands, but a representation of what *can* or logically *must* be. The memory upsets the basic order, edits, cuts and makes what is real stand out – the movements of the cinematic camera are symbolic of these mental mechanisms. In his choice of certain fragments of movement, Degas adopted a system for underscoring the fleetingness of the moment, and hence laid the foundations for an art form that is based more on analysis than on emotions.

Where Manet excelled in gleaning the most subtle alterations in the play of light, Degas succeeded in capturing the slightest detail of a movement – it is easy to understand why he was so tempted by sculpture. This is also the reason why he chose the theme of dance and sculpted the series of ballerina figures. Unconcerned about demonstrating a moment from history (which was Manet's concern), Degas aimed to catch the entirety of human gesture. He is a witness at a higher level, an artist utterly absorbed in the question of movement. And in fact the real subject of his art becomes just that – movement for movement's sake.

He foreshadowed a modern tendency to convey mobility by portraying a real movement, and succeeded in enhancing reality with another reality of his own fraught with layers of meaning.

Photography appealed strongly to Degas and he experimented extensively with the medium, staging new situations, exploring different forms of composition which he would later express to greater advantage in painting.

Japanese prints also caught his fancy, as an entire generation was introduced to this extraordinary art form. In 1856, Bracquemond found a volume of illustrations by Hokusai and showed it to his friends. By 1862, the Orient had become highly fashionable in artistic circles. On her return from Japan, a certain Mme. Desoye opened a shop under the porticoes of Rue Rivoli called "La Porte Chinoise".

James Whistler was among the first to begin a collection of Chinese porcelain and costumes. He even posed for Fantin-Latour in a kimono. There is a trace of Japanese art in Degas' 1868 portrait of James Tissot and in Manet's portrait of Emile Zola. Writers and painters flocked to Mme. Desoye's shop – Manet, Fantin-Latour, Baudelaire, the de Goncourt brothers and, of course, Degas, who recognized the novelty and great potential of the Japanese print.

He marveled at the graceful style of line, the force of the decisive and uncorrected brushstrokes, the highly original balance and the way the subject was displaced to one side. But rather than indulge in *japonaiseries*, Degas used his new knowledge of the Eastern sensibility to rewrite his vision of the Western world. *From Italy to Spain, from Greece to Japan, the procedure is much the same: it is a question of synthesizing the essential data of life. The rest is up to the eye and the hand of the artist.*

(1) Raymond Cogniat.
(2) Jean Cocteau in *Le Secret Professionnel*.

A PAINFUL CHANGE

In the second half of the 19th century, the art of painting, which was so tied to the representation of reality and to revealing its secrets, abruptly broke free from its bonds and embraced new possibilities. But these same openings put an end to certain basic needs that had guaranteed its perpetuity. Here was a new philosophy of painting, a form of expression detached from reality, living off itself, no longer obliged to listen to the world but creating new ones of its own, no longer dependent on strictly visible data but on intimate impulses. And as painting drifted into an anarchical realm beyond formulas, the introduction of new techniques launched a strictly visual analysis of reality.

The drama facing painters after the memorable years in which not only their social role was questioned but also the validity of their tools, was to reconcile the new freedom of visual idiom with the inherited desire to endow the canvas with what the world lay before them. It is symptomatic that, down through the ages, the painters' approach to reality was fired by a basic desire to share their joys, their hardships, their beliefs even. Once the *image* of the world was no longer the heart of painting, painting was slowly destroyed. New prejudices were to be encountered, inevitably (and they are not lacking in the 20th century) but the artists of the 19th century, and in particular the generation that first experienced the invention of photography, felt the full effects of its introduction as a visual medium.

Degas, Manet and Cézanne were the first victims and the first heroes of the change, of this breach with the past. They had to create the new from the old, to reconcile fifty centuries of human figurative expression with the desire (however confused) for a new perception of the world on an instinctive level. The desire for a new instantaneity was accompanied by a more acute notion of time that passed, that transformed, that modeled death within life itself.

The drama Degas faced was similar to that of Ravel, who found himself at a threshold of the old musical world, with the utter novelty of Debussy's inventive genius before him. Degas was a pupil of Ingres, whereas Claude Monet was the architect of a form of painting that no longer had a subject, a form of expression left to its own devices. For his part, Degas, who was tolerated with difficulty by his friends at the café for his sudden manias and flights of enthusiasm for mediocre art (to the extent that some asked themselves whether he could discern at all), was forever torn between contrasting positions.

As an admirer of Ingres, Degas was not unmoved by the subtle mysteries of Eugène Delacroix, by his inebriated coloring. While he was modern in his choice of subject matter, Degas continued to aspire to a Classical vision. Hostile to theory, he screened himself with aphorisms. And since straightforward painting, that pure expression of visual delight, was gradually being usurped by the moral and intellectual speculations between art as expression and art as reflection, the type of subject matter Degas forged did not allow him to cast aside the old principles of his *métier*. Meanwhile he envied Manet's self-assurance and sophisticated audacity. Critics remarked on his vast technical prowess, but he would rather have been a poet. An inveterate agitator, Degas was branded as a bad lot and relegated to the bachelor sanctuary of his apartment. Degas realized that painting had changed, inexorably, that it was no longer a representation of something, but an end in itself.

Photography taught him that one's vision of reality could be altered at whim, and he created a new art form that he continued to people with figures borrowed from traditional painting. He may have been considered a realist, but he was really aiming for the pure poetry of matter made sensation. In this, the ill-natured but eminently droll Degas had completed his most serious work to date. Willpower had won over emotion, verging almost on abstraction, the abstraction of gesture. Toward the end of his existence, virtually blind, Degas would finally discover the excitement of the inebriated line let loose on the paper; the brushstroke that evolved into a band of gleaming color on the canvas.

In a characteristically terse exchange of opinions, when Gustave Moreau asked Degas whether he intended to renovate art through dance, the latter replied "Why, do you hope to renovate it through jewelry then?" As the end neared, his work became a confused blaze of color. As soon as he found a means of working faster, based on pastels, the old master could not help turning back to his old themes. He worked in stages, his figures became more assertive. One is reminded of Giacometti's anguished striving to apprehend the intimacy of his objects. Degas, collected and determined, continued to get closer to his elusive reality. He did not aim to capture it as the Impressionists did, who entrusted themselves to inspiration and the impulse of the moment, he would define it himself. The pictures that followed the first series of works so laboriously constructed had all the appearance of sketches.

The strikingly limited range of subject matter in Degas' work perhaps harbingered the complete suppression of subject matter that took place in the 20th century. Alternatively, it denotes the gradual substitution of a form of painting that is focused on a subject, for a form of painting in which the subject is merely a pretext.

The nudes and horses that kept recurring in Degas' work are like the graphic marks of today's painters, signs reduced to their simplest form. In Degas, the sign is translated in the muscular vigor of a horse in the race; the physical effort of the dancer, or the forms of a woman busy washing herself. And everywhere there are signs of curves, bodies in different states of tension, different positions of precariousness. More than a painter of human beings, Degas was foremost a painter of body movement, translated into the races, into dance and into physical effort. This progressive intimacy with the human body is like a transposition of Degas' psychological and sexual problems. His was a disturbing, ambiguous vision, but one which quickly goes beyond the subject itself to harness something

that could not be fixed on the canvas, because that was not its purpose. Its purpose was to capture the very dynamism of life.

As a man projected into the 20th century, Degas bore witness to the profound changes that occurred around him as his society discovered modernity. He tried to adapt to the changing era, of which he was an intelligent and docile product. As Fernand Léger was to do some decades later, Degas drew on certain elements of his time to create a grammar of form that would suffice unto itself. In this way, Degas is perhaps the Léger of the 19th century – a strong idealist, a biased witness. He was above all a painter and, as such, keen to conjugate the eternal force of human gesture, in the clearest of terms. Through his observation of humankind, he would inject his canvases with life itself.

Life is not a set of speculations but a race toward something definite. Without realizing it, Degas translated this research and its evolution toward the final desperation, the errant vacuity and whatever was useless, vain or disillusioned.

He led his art from pure idea toward sensation, from idealism toward an appearance of realism, from perfection to approximation, from the formulation of convention to the statement of necessity.

1834	*Degas is born on July 19. His father is a bank director; his mother, née Husson, was originally from New Orleans.* Revolt of the silk workers in Lyons. Louis-Philippe tightens his regime following Fieschi's assassination attempt.
1837	Queen Victoria's succession to the throne of Great Britain.
1839	The Opium War breaks out between China and Great Britain.
1840	Birth of Monet.
1841	Birth of Renoir.
1845	*Degas attends the Lycée Louis le Grand. Makes friends with Henri Rouart.*
1847	*Death of Degas' mother. Thanks to his father he discovers museum-going.*
1848	Revolution in France. Proclamation of the Second Republic. Marx publishes his *Communist Manifesto.* Birth of Gauguin.
1851	Coup d'état of December 2nd gives full power to Louis-Napoleon.
1852	*Degas sets up his first studio in the family home.* Napoleon III, Emperor of France.

1853	*Degas copies works he sees in museums.* Birth of van Gogh.
1854	*Degas studies under Lamothe, a follower of Ingres. Visit to Naples.* The Crimean War. Siege of Sebastopol.
1855	*Degas is admitted to the Ecole des Beaux-Arts. Makes friends with Bonnat and Fantin-Latour.*
1856	*Trips to Rome, Naples and Florence. His "Notebooks."*
1858	*Trips to Rome, Florence; carries out his first studies for the Belleli family portrait.*
1859	Birth of Seurat.
1860	*Paintings with historical subjects.*
1861	*Degas paints* Semiramis Building Babylon. Civil War in the United States (1861-1865). The Archduke Maximilian is executed by a firing squad in Mexico. Ingres paints *Le Bain Turc* (at the age of 81).

1862	*Friendship with Manet.*
1863	Salon des Refusés. Manet paints *Le Déjeuner sur l'Herbe.*
1864	Birth of Toulouse-Lautrec. The French win the right to strike. First International.
1865	*Misadventures in the City of Orleans.* Manet paints his *Olympia.*
1867	The de Goncourt brothers publish their *Manette Salomon.* The double monarchy of the Austro-Hungarian empire consolidates the Germanic domination of Europe. Deaths of Baudelaire and Ingres.
1868	*Degas paints his* Mademoiselle Fiocre. Birth of Vuillard.
1869	Birth of Matisse. Manet paints his *Balcony.* First appearances of the Impressionist technique. Opening of the Suez Canal.
1870	War between France and Germany. Fantin-Latour paints his *L'Atelier des Batignolles. Degas enlists.*

1871	The Paris Commune.
1872	*Degas starts to haunt the Opéra wings (rue le Peletier). Trip to New Orleans:* The Cotton Office. Obligatory military service in France.
1873	The fall of Thiers. MacMahon president of the Republic.
1874	First Impressionist exhibition.
1875	Death of Corot.
1876	Second Impressionist exhibition.
1877	Fall of MacMahon.
1878	Publication of T. Duret's work, *Les Peintres Impressionistes.*
1879	Death of Daumier. 14 July declared a national holiday.

1880	Death of Flaubert. *Degas travels to Spain and does engravings in collaboration with Mary Cassatt.* State schools are established in France, exclusively non-religious.
1881	*Degas exhibits his first piece of sculpture. He increasingly uses pastels in his other works.* Birth of Picasso. Terrorism in Russia. Alexander II is assassinated.
1882	*Degas frequently returns to the themes of "women ironing" and the "milliner's shop."*
1883	Death of Manet. Conquest of colonial territories in Africa.
1885	*Degas and Gauguin meet. Degas starts to have sight problems.*
1886	The Douanier Rousseau gains notoriety. The eighth and last Impressionist exhibition. *Degas exhibits a series of "nude women bathing, washing themselves, drying themselves, combing their hair and having it combed by others."*
1888	William II crowned Emperor of Germany.
1889	*Degas tours Spain with Boldini.*
1890	Death of van Gogh.

1891	First exhibition of the "Nabis." Gauguin is in Tahiti.
1893	*Degas does his first "monotypes." He has increasing difficulties with his sight.* Inauguration of the Vollard gallery.
1895	Birth of the CGT (Confédération Général du Travail – association of French trade unions).
1897	*Degas makes his pilgrimage to Montauban to see Ingres' work.*
1898	The Dreyfus scandal. *Degas visits St-Valéry-sur-Somme.*
1899	Nabis exhibition. Death of Sisley.
1901	Death of Toulouse-Lautrec.
1905	First revolution in Russia.
1912	Death of Henri Rouart. *Degas moves out of his apartment in Rue Victor Massé. He commands high prices at the public auctions.*
1914	Juarès assassinated. Start of World War I.
1917	October Revolution in Russia. *September 27, Degas dies at the age of 84.*

Written by the Artist

Degas' Notebooks at the Cabinet des Estampes. *Gazette des Beaux-Arts*, 1921.

Lettres inédites de Degas	Revue de Paris, 1921.
Lettres de Degas, recueillies et annotées par Marcel Guérin	Preface by Daniel Halévy, Grasset, 1931.
Huit sonnets de Degas	Preface by Jean Nepveu-Degas, La Jeune Parque, 1946.

MONOGRAPHS AND CRITICAL STUDIES

M. Liebermann	*Degas*, Berlin 1902.
P.A. Lemoisne	*Degas*, Libraire Central des Beaux-Arts, Paris 1921.
	Degas et son-oeuvre (4 volumes), Paris 1946.
P. Lafond	*Degas* (2 volumes), Floury, Paris 1918.
H. Hertz	*Degas*, Alcan, Paris 1922.
J. Meier-Graefe	*Degas*, Munich 1920.
François Fosca	*Degas*, Albert Messein, Paris 1921.
Gustave Coquiot	*Degas*, Ollendorf, Paris 1924.
Ambroise Vollard	*Degas*, Crès, Paris 1924.
Paul Jamot	*Degas*, Editions Gazette des Beaux-Arts, Paris 1927.
	Degas, Skira, Geneva 1939.
J. B. Manson	*The Life and Work of Degas*, London 1927.
A. André	*Degas*, Braun, Paris 1924.
Georges Rivière	*Degas, Bourgeois de Paris*, Floury, Paris 1935.
G. Grappe	*Degas*, Plon, Paris 1936.
Camille Mauclair	*Degas*, Hypérion, Paris 1937.
Denis Rouart	*Degas a la recherche de sa technique*, Floury, Paris 1946.
	Monotypes de Degas, Paris 1948.
	Degas, Braun, Paris 1948.
Jean Leymarie	*Les Degas du Louvre*, Paris 1948.
Jacques Lassaigne	*Degas*, Hypérion, Paris 1948.
W. Hausenstein	*Degas*, Berne 1948.
Lillian Browse	*Degas's Dancers*, Faber & Faber, London 1949.
D. Catton Rich	*Degas*, Abrams, New York 1951.
Robert Rey	*Degas*, Somogy, Paris 1952.
D. Cooper	*Pastels de Degas*, Basle 1952.
René Huyghe	*Degas*, Flammarion, Paris 1953.
Pierre Cabanne	*Degas*, Pierre Tisné, Paris 1957.
Jean Bouret	*Degas*, Somogy, Paris 1965.
Denis Rouart and M. Stevanovic	*Renoir et Degas inconnus*, Cercle d'art, Paris 1966.
Flammarion, eds.	*Tout l'oeuvre peint de Degas*, Paris 1974.

MEMOIRS AND ACCOUNTS

Duranty	*Réalisme*, Paris 1856-57.
	La nouvelle peinture, Dentu, Paris 1876.
	Le pays des arts, Charpentier, Paris 1881.
J. K. Huysmans	*Certains*, Paris 1889.
	L'art moderne, Plon, Paris 1908.
	Journal des Goncourt, Charpentier, Paris 1891.
Jacques Emile Blanche	*Essais et portraits*, Paris 1912.
Marice Denis	*Henry Lérolle et ses amis*, Paris 1931.
Daniel Halévy	*Pays parisien*, Grasset, Paris 1932.
Ambroise Vollard	*Souvenirs d'un marchand de tableaux*, Albin, Paris 1952.
Paul Valéry	*Degas, danse, dessin*, Paris 1938.
Jean Fèvre	*Mon oncle Degas*, Geneva 1949.